A GHOSTLY GUIDE
TO
WEST VIRGINIA

By

James Foster Robinson

Dedicated to Dan and all the Ghosts Hunters of West Virginia

THANKS TO

My wife Betty for her encouragement and support, Kevin and Gean at work for reading the text and their encouragement, Ken at work for his contribution of a story, and the Smith family next door for allowing me to photograph their carved pumpkins at Halloween. The cover shot is from one of the pictures.

TABLE OF CONTENTS

Mountain, Number 2 Mine, Nutter Fort

INTRODUCTION

Since moving to West Virginia, I have seen some ghosts. Moore Fork is located in the Big Otter area. My wife's family had a farm there where she grew up. When I first visited the valley in February 2005 with Betty, I was immediately struck by a feeling that the valley was alive, and that I had been there before. I also felt something rushing down from the hilltops as if to greet me - welcome me back again. People who have seen a picture of me taken in the Moore Fork valley, remark how much I seemed to be at home there. Every time I visit Moore Fork, I do not feel like a stranger. I told Betty that I felt that the area was haunted or had a spirit there. She then told me about the haunted house near where she had lived. When you walked by it, you could hear a baby crying where none existed. They say that a dead baby had been buried under the corner of that house and was crying for attention. Local folks would avoid it when ever possible.

I travel Trace Fork Road off I-119 to go and from work. At least twice, on foggy nights, at the same spot, I have glimpsed in my headlights what appears to be a wolf running on the road straight at my car. It disappears just before I would hit it! My wife says there used to be a man living in the area who had a tame wolf for a pet. Was that it's ghost I was seeing?

I grew up in a haunted house in Prescott, Ontario. While living in Kingston, Ontario and writing about the area's unusual history for a weekly newspaper, I was called upon at various times to check out some hauntings. While working a security officer in Ontario, British Columbia and West Virginia, I encountered situations that could only be described as ghostly appearances.

It seems that West Virginia, itself, is full of ghosts. The hills and hollows (pronounced "hollers") have many spectral residents. The people of West Virginia, living in the still wild and semi-isolated mountains and hills, told of the dwellers in the hills. Things that, they say, would awake at dark and prowl around outside the mountain folk's homes. The Irish called them "the Sidhe" while the Cherokee had a tongue-twisting name that meant "the little men". It is said that these dwellers in the hills used our dreams to speak to us. Perhaps they are also the generators of our nightmares. Maybe they are responsible for the many weird things and in particular ghosts, that happen in West Virginia.

I created this guide for those who are interested in ghosts whether they believe in them or not. This guide is not an in-depth investigation of haunted places but an introduction to the subject. As such I have not elaborated on each ghostly appearance but gave you just enough detail to pique your morbid curiosity. I have also tried to provide you with some tools to help you start you on your ghostly quest, if you are so inclined. Sit down in a comfortable chair, lock your doors and turn on ALL your lights and start reading. If you hear strange sounds, pay no attention. Keep on reading. If you see something out of the corner of you eye, ignore it. Just keep on reading. You will be might be ok...maybe... Just Maybe!!!

CHAPTER A

Agnes Street see **Parkersburg**

Alum Creek, Lincoln and Kanawha Counties
Alum Creek is a quiet, little community on Alum Creek where it enters the Coal River off US Route 119. Part of the community is in Kanawha County and the other in Lincoln County. The area does have one unusual resident. Alum Creek Missionary Baptist Cemetery sits on the hill behind the Alum Creek Missionary Baptist Church. Visitors to this cemetery have encountered him - sort of! They have seen an elderly man wandering around the cemetery apparently very confused. When they approach to help him, the elderly man disappears into thin air.

Alum Creek Missionary Baptist Cemetery see **Alum Creek**

Ambrose Hill Phantom see **Parkersburg**

Apartment 16 see **White Sulphur Springs**

Athens, Mercer County
Athens is a small town in Mercer County with a population of 1,102 in the year 2000. The community is a part of the Bluefield, WV-VA metropolitan area. The house at 137 Sammy Street in Athens is said to be haunted. The front door in the living room would open and close by itself. There are "dead" areas in the house where cell phones will not work. Giggling can be heard in an adjacent bedroom when no one is in it. Some residents have not been able to stay long in the house because of their strange experiences. Students and staff living on campus at Concord College in Athens, Mercer County, have reported horrible nightmares, apparitions and feelings of a mischievous presence. No one seems to know who or what causes it.

CHAPTER B

Babcock State Park, Fayette County

Babcock State Park lies adjacent to the New River Gorge National Park in Fayette County. One of its popular spots to visit is the Glade Creek Grist Mill. Less than a mile from the mill, a woman was brutally murdered in Cabin #13 by her preacher husband in 1996. The minister, when arrested and charged with murder, claimed they had been attacked by a masked man who killed his wife. The woman now haunts the spot. Her spectral form has been seen in and around Cabin # 13. A paranormal investigation group took a picture of the cabin which shows what they say to be ectoplasm, floating upwards on the porch. At the time the picture was taken, no one saw the ectoplasm. Is this the ghost of the murdered woman seeking revenge on her husband?

Bagwell Ave see Nutter Fort

Barboursville, Cabell County

Barboursville, in the Huntington-Ashland metro area, has a relatively new jail which opened in 2003. But the Western Regional Jail is already haunted! Staff have experienced strange things both inside and outside the jail. And I am not talking about the inmates. For one thing, doors have often been heard being opened and closed. Investigations found that it was not the cell doors. Could all the paranormal activity be related to an small old family cemetery that was moved when the new jail was built? Maybe the restless spirits are trying to open the cell doors to let the unwanted guests out?

A house on Childers Road in Barboursville has an unseen resident. Well, more than one! Something walks around the attic and keeps pushing the gable vent out from the inside. Someone unseen climbs the ladder in the closet. A disembodied female voice tells the man of the house to wash the dishes. The TV turns on by itself as does the lights and the water in the kitchen. Dishes placed in one spot would be found moved elsewhere as if some unseen housekeeper was cleaning things up. Childers Road has another ghost hanging around. A little boy, who drowned during a flood while riding his bike on the road, still likes to rides his bike at night during flood season.

Visitors to the Swan Cemetery in Barboursville, Cabell County, have experienced the weird feeling of not being alone when there was no one else in the area. When they took pictures, unexplained anomalies showed up on their developed prints. Maybe the spirits in that graveyard did not like having their sleep disturbed.

Barrackville, Marion County

A mine explosion at Barrackville killed a number of miners including one colored worker names Jeremy Walker. Now Jeremy was a well-liked and friendly work companion in life and even in death. He had always helped the others to fill their quota by help loading their carts. He did not stop even though he was killed. The miners always met their quota for Jeremy would fill their carts when they were not looking. They were not scared for they could hear his playful laugh. When hand loading was replaced by mechanized methods, Jeremy figured his work was done and he apparently passed on to the "Great Mine in the Sky".

Battle of Rich Mountain see **Isner Creek**

"Beamer" see **Centralia**

"Beech Bottom Lady" see **Scarbo**

Beach Fork Road, Wayne County
Residents on Beach Fork Road near Lavalette used to hear a strange screaming in the evenings. At first they thought it was a panther. Gunshots were fired to scare it off but the screaming did not stop. The screaming continue long into the night, sometimes all night long. One day some of the local kids found a small cemetery with about seven headstones in it. One of the stones with a woman's name on it had fallen or been turned over. The boys put it back up. The screaming was never heard again. Did the woman, who was buried there, get really upset because her stone was knocked over? And did she stop screaming when the boys put it back up for her?

Beckley, Raleigh County
Beckley in Raleigh County is a bit of a hot bed for restless ghosts. The Soldier's Memorial Theater and Arts Center in Beckley now houses public offices and serves as a community center. But for years the old theatre was haunted by a gentleman ghost cloaked in gray. His appearances was often accompanied by children's laughter and ethereal music. Those in the know say that the strange happenings are the result of an accident during the construction of the building. Does the old gray gentleman ghost still put in an appearance?

"The Lady in Red" is the resident ghost at the County Courthouse in Beckley, Raleigh County. This spooky apparition wears a red dress. Hence her name, silly! She visits the jurors room often as well as putting in an occasional appearance in the court room. Why she is there and what she wants is a complete mystery.

Old Beckley Junior High use to be a hospital during the civil war. A young nurse named Hanna was killed there and she can still be heard moaning over her untimely demise. Also, footsteps from unseen people can be heard moving up and down the halls.

Beckley County Courthouse see **Beckley**

Beckley Junior High see Beckley

Benton's Ferry see Fairmont

Benton's Hill see **Vinegar Hill, Copper Hollow**

Berkeley Springs, Morgan County
A prince of American Commerce and a one time ambassador to England , Maryland businessman Samuel Taylor Suit, built a castle in 1885 in Berkeley Springs, Morgan County for his true love and new bride, Rosa. The castle was modeled after Castle Berkeley outside Bath, England. After Samuel died, Rosa consoled herself by throwing lavish and expensive parties. She blew the fortune left her by her late husband and was forced to sell the castle to settle her debts. But the riches-to-rags widow did not forget her castle even after she died. When it was opened to the public, visitors reported seeing a ghostly figure of a woman like Rosa roaming the halls. Strange shadows have appeared and disappeared to unbelieving eyes. Unwilling ears have heard odd noises. The ghost of a young girl giggles and sings her way throughout the castle halls. Colonel Suit, wearing his distinctive long-tail tuxedo, roams the castle, perhaps looking for Rosa to get her to explain why she flittered away his fortune. Last but not least, an Indian warrior, long dead but still alive in ghostly form, guards his tribe's buried treasure near Berkeley Springs.

Besoco, Raleigh County
The now abandoned Old Stoco Jr. High in Besoco, Raleigh County, is haunted. People alone in the school at night have heard voices, footsteps, echoes, and the sound of people moving in the halls. Strange writings, thought to be from witchcraft, and other unexplainable things, have appeared mysteriously on its walls. Some say it is just graffiti from bored teens. But no one has been caught doing it. Wherever you go in the school you get an eerie feeling of unseen eyes watching you. All this paranormal activity is attributed to the ghost of a boy who was accidentally pushed into the bleachers one night during a game. He split his head open and died in route to the hospital. He seems to be very unhappy about that. You can hear him dribbling his ball and the screeching of his tennis shoes on the floor. The gym was cold at times and ghost seekers have seen a ghostly figure float through the doorway and out into the hall. Maybe it was the ghostly basketball player, finished with his game and heading for the showers.

Beta Theta Pi House see **Morgantown**

Bethany, Brooke County
Phillips Hall at Bethany College in Bethany, Brooke County, has a permanent student, a ghost called "Sarah". She apparently loved college live so much that she hangs around the women's dorm, borrowing things from the other girls and hides them.

No ghosts have appeared, that I know of, in the Bethany Cemetery in Bethany, Brooke County. But visitors to the cemetery have reported feeling trapped and also an eerie presence - of what, it is not known. Perhaps the trapped feeling may result from the five foot high limestone wall that surrounds the place.

Bethany Cemetery see **Bethany**

Bethany College see **Bethany**

Betts House, Calhoun County
A troop of Civil War Calvary still rides to battle on top of a mountain across from the Betts

house three miles from Grantsville. You can hear the tramping of spectral horses and the rattling of invisible sabers just before they appear at full gallop and heading straight for you! Run for your life! Also see Grantsville, Calhoun County

Big Bend Tunnel see **Talcott**

Big Branch, Wyoming County
Big Branch is located on Route 97, northeast of Hanover. Someone long dead is still hanging around a woods near here. In what was once an Indian burial ground, some people have encountered a long haired man who states that he is the last and please let him rest. They say he is still not at rest. He still haunts the woods near Big Branch.

Big Branch Hollow, Boone County
In the 1970's, a trailer burnt down in Big Branch Hollow near Greenview. A family of three were killed. Later a house was built on the property and is now said to be hunted by a woman wearing a long flowing night gown standing at the top of the steps to the place. Other strange things have also happened in that house, but you will have to ask the owners what they were. Do not be surprised if they do not tell you.

Big Fork Hollow, Kanawha County
A young woman and her baby haunt a house in Big Fork Hollow on Frame Road in Elkview. She appears to be about twenty years old and wears old style clothes. People have seen her appear out of nowhere and enter the house. A baby cries just before she appears and stops when she enters the house. A search of the building by witnesses have found nothing. Is she, after all these years, still taking care of her crying baby?

"Black Thing, The" see **Johnstown**

Blennerhassett Hotel see **Parkersburg**

Blennerhassett Island, Wood County
Blennerhassett Island in the Ohio river near Parkersburg, Wood County has a long history. It is also haunted! Margret Blennerhassett and her two children still walk the island long after they passed away. Often you can smell perfume when no one is around - that is - no one who is wearing that type of perfume.

Bluefield, Mercer County
Mahood Hall at Bluefield State College, Bluefield, Mercer County, is another institute of higher learning that is haunted. The spirit of a young girl roams its halls and basement. Do not doze off in the building. When you wake up you might just see the eyes of the young girl's ghost staring at you!

The dead are still restless at Wade Elementary School in Bluefield, Mercer County. A woman was decapitated there and three children dropped dead for no apparent reason. Ghostly children still run through the school even though it is closed and locked.

Several of the dead buried in the old part of Woodlawn Cemetery in Bluewell, Mercer County do not want to be disturbed. They will tell you to go away!

Blumehaven Inn see **Fayette County**

Board Tree Tunnel, Marshall County
During the construction of the Board Tree Tunnel, many workers were killed in accidents, disease or being hit by trains. A section boss had the great misfortune to be hit and killed by a train the very day the tunnel was finished. There after his ghost often walked the tracks with one of his living friends. Trainmen often saw a light at the opening of the tunnel as they approached. The light would suddenly vanish when they arrived at the entrance.

Boiling Springs, Wood County
Once upon a time, a hotel called Boiling Springs sat about fourteen miles down US 50 east of Parkersburg. Once a popular site, people now avoid it as it is haunted by two men and woman. The hapless men, fighting over the woman, both fell over a cliff and died. The distraught woman jumped after them over the cliff to her death. They say that you can hear still weird, unexplained noises at night.

Bolivar, Jefferson County
A Civil War battle took place at Bolivar near Harper's Ferry. Some soldiers from that conflict are buried in a cemetery near Harper's Ferry Middle School. That cemetery is haunted. Visitors to it have encountered Civil War soldiers who appeared confused and stared at a grave. The soldiers even asked what the date was before disappearing. Inspection of the grave reveals a picture of the solders just seen there. The confused soldiers were ghosts!

Boone County
On one of the back roads in Boone County, a woman with paint and markings on her face has been see late at night. Those who see her have been scared out of their wits. No one, however knows who she is, what she is doing there and why.

Booth's Creek, Marion County
A man from Pennsylvania was murdered on a road by Booth's Creek near Bobtown and Monongah at the time of the Civil War. The victim did not like it and, there after, showed his dissatisfaction by sitting on a coffin as it rose up out of the side of the road. The ghost and coffin then floated across the road and disappeared. The ghost apparently tired of his antics for he and his coffin has not been seen since 1935. Or have they?

Boreman Hall see **Morgantown**

Boys Industrial School see **Lakin**

Brandon Road see **Huntington**

Bridgeport, Harrison County

The family living at 707 Stout Street in Bridgeport have an unwanted house guest. It is known as the 707 Phantom. A dark figure often stands at the foot of the bed in one of the bedrooms. Another shadowy figure -maybe the same one - stands on the mantle of the fire place in the living room. Demonic laughter often resounds through the house. Know one knows who or what the 707 Phantom is!

Something dark must have happened in the Meadowbrook Mall area of Bridgeport, Harrison County. The ghostly forms of three men dressed in robes are often seen crossing the road late at night. The figure in front is carrying a torch while the other two following have their arms in their sleeves. This spectacle does not happen just around Halloween but apparently any night of the year.

Two young men, who driving down East Olive Street in Bridgeport one night, had an unexpected passenger. When they came to a stop sign, the driver had a bizarre feeling. Suddenly, sitting to the right of the passenger in the front seat was a younger man where the widow normally would be. The driver and the new passenger stared at each other. The ghost disappeared after the car started to move down the street. The mysterious passenger has never been seen again. Or has he? Have you run into him on East Olive Street some dark and lonely night?

Brooksville, Calhoun County

A haunted house once existed on the edge of the small town of Brooksville. Those, with the courage or stupidly - as some might say - to check the house out around midnight, just might hear someone or something dragging chains down the hall, down the stairs and outside. They say that a very bad husband kept his wife chained up to prevent her from going out. Then one night he killed her and buried her in the yard. Seems like she was still trying to go out, chains and all. The house is long torn down, but I wonder if you went there at midnight, would you still hear the chains?

Bud Mountain, Wyoming County

Bud Mountain at Bud in Wyoming County has a several ghosts hanging about there. The most famous is old man Burg Hammon. Burg, a peddler, died when he drove his buggy over the mountain at this point. If you start up the first steep hill at the bottom of the mountain at night when the moon is full, you can hear him playing his fiddle. If you don't, just call out "Burg Hammon let us hear your pretty music!". He will play for you. Then relax and enjoy the music. Many years ago, George Sizemore who lived in a house (now torn down) at the bottom of the hill, was killed by his stepson. But George is still there on Bud mountain. He has been seen standing over people's bed at night or staring out the windows of the house. Often, when his widow was walking home after visiting her boyfriend, George would walk in front of her. A ghostly couple, Mr. And Mrs. Eastridge, also haunted the same house. Mrs. Eastridge would stand at the foot of one of the beds. Then the bed springs would creak and some unseen someone would walk into the kitchen, stop at the sink and then return to the bed. Then the bedsprings would creak again. Was old Mrs. Eastridge getting a drink of water every night? Mr. Eastridge was killed, possibly murdered, working in the fields. Before, dying he crawled back to the house where he still hangs around. What looked like a dog was spotted one night crawling towards the house. As it got closer, it looked more like a man. As this man stepped onto the porch, the occupants of the house retired quickly inside and barred the door. A local man, who had been shot and killed after arguing with another man over a gun, has been seem occasionally by a coal heap near the house. The family, who lived in the house before it was torn down, once saw what looked like a funeral in progress at the local cemetery. A number of unknown people were standing around a man digging a grave. When the family inquired of their neighbors who had died, no one knew. When they went back to the cemetery, there was no one there or no fresh grave!

"Burg Hammon" see **Bud Mountain**

Burnt House, Ritchie County
If you are traveling on the Staunton-Parkersburg Turnpike near the village of Burnt House sixteen miles west of Glenville on a damp foggy night, you just might be a spectator to the spectacle of the specter of a black slave woman dancing over the ruins of a long burned down tavern. Then she might drift to the accompaniment of a plaintive moan out over Deadman's hollow. This ghost was once a living person named Delores, who was the lover of Mr. Harris who owned the tavern. Harris decided to seek his fortune out west when the neighborhood got a little too hot for him. Many thought that he had something to do with the death of several peddlers whose bodies were found in Needman's Hollow. He sold the tavern in 1852 and Delores with it. Delores was, needless to say, devastated! Shortly there after the tavern caught fire mysteriously. Delores was seen dancing in the flames. For thirty years she was seen dancing in ghostly flames on damp foggy nights at that spot. Then one night, the same day, they say, that Harris was hanged in Texas for robbery, a terrible electric storm lashed the village of Burnt House and its valley. Delores never danced again.

CHAPTER C

Cabin # 13 see **Babcock State Park**

Cabin Creek, Kanawha County
The Hale House, a historical site located near Cabin Creek, Kanawha County, has a permanent ghostly resident - a man still roams the ground and the house, some think unjustly, seeking justice for his murder. Unjustly because he was reputed to be abusive towards his wife. She and her husband lived there with an uncle. One night, someone got tired of the husband's abuse and killed him. An investigation never found out who the murderer was. Abusive husbands beware! You too could end up as an insubstantial specter chained for eternity to some old house.

"Cale Bett" see **Grantsville**

Calhoun County
There is a little white house five miles out of a town and two miles up a holler in Calhoun County. The only house on that branch of the holler, it was haunted once upon a time. But you would not think it would be haunted looking at it. The place was a little, white, one story house with a sun porch. But it was definitely haunted as a family that moved into it in the 1970's found out. The house was "alive with ghosts!" During the day, galloping horses and men yelling could be heard where neither horses or men were to be found. A car could be heard pulling up to the house. No car could be seen! Someone would slam two of the car's doors and then walk across the sun porch to the front door. No person could be seen! Spooky! One bedroom was always cold. People staying in the room felt that they were always being watched. One night a light was seen at the bedroom window. It grew bigger until it turned into a face. This was nothing compared to the shadow! A man, solid black in form, wearing a fedora and a long coat was often seen in the house. He exuded a feeling of cruel evilness. Several families lived in the house for short times. Then the house was completely remodeled by one owner and the scary activity seemed to cease - or did it?

Campbells Creek, Kanawha County
A house in Campbells Creek in eastern Kanawha County had a restless spirit as a resident. It liked to make a clanking noise like someone hitting a grate with a poker where a fireplace used to be. The sound of a door opening, followed by the sound of footsteps, have been heard when no one could have made them. The strange happenings continued until the father of the family died in 1990. Was the ghostly resident trying to get his attention?

Capels Road, McDowell County
A S.A.F.E house, once located on the old Capels Road near Capels, had an unwanted guest. Whoever or whatever it was kept on breaking things - the CD in the CD player and glasses of

water for instance. Someone could be heard walking the halls after midnight. At first a search of the building found no one. Then, when the sound was heard again, witnesses saw a man six foot four in bare feet, long black hair, dressed in old bear skin pants and with funny painting on his chest, arms and face. The man, thus caught, yelled loudly and promptly disappeared. Other people staying in the house have had the frightening misfortune to make his acquaintance. The specter is thought to be an Indian who had been buried on what was a sacred Indian burial site before the house was built.

Capon Bridge, Hampshire County

There is an old grave yard west of Capon Bridge on a hill off Route 50 with a little used dirt road running behind it into the woods. People, who have wandered down that road at night, have reported hearing the sounds of laughter and the crackle of a camp fire. There was no one around and there was no campfire in sight. Then they heard footsteps from unseen people following them. Suddenly ghostly faces appeared among the trees and the hapless travelers lit out of there for home. Who or what made the spooky noise? Who did the spectral faces belong to? Were they soldiers from the Civil war still hanging around?

Capitol High School see Charleston

Capitol Plaza Theatre see Charleston

Carriage Trail see Charleston

Cass, Pocahontas County

An old refurbished home in Cass in Pocahontas County on the Greenbrier River is haunted. Who, or whatever it is, continually opens and slams doors at night. Sometimes it feels as if the house is shaking and the glass is breaking. Windows in cars parked outside the house have been mysteriously shattered. People have woken to find a man standing beside them trying hard to lift them. When they call out, the man disappears. Someone sure does not want anyone to be in that house.

Cass Railroad see Elkins

Centralia, Braxton County

A train around 1890 ran over and beheaded a man known locally in the Centralia area as Beamer. Today, or rather tonight, if you are in or near a deep cut near the village of Centralia thirteen miles up the Elk River from Sutton, and the moon is out, and if it is a particular night of the year and a particular time (Don't ask me which ones!), then you just might still see a gray ghost leading a headless man through the cut. The headless man, of course, is Beamer, and guess what? The gray ghost is apparently Beamer's family guardian ghost! They say Beamer used to claim that his ancestors came to live on the Earth from the moon after a meteor destroyed their home there. The last sighting of Beamer was during the depression when two hunters spied Beamer and his ghostly assistant. Beamer was clutching a skull under his arm. Did they finally find his head?

Ceredo, Wayne County

The Civil War still lingers in a house in Ceredo, Wayne County. Ramsdell House is said to have been the last stop for slaves in one of the underground railway route before they crossed into Ohio and freedom. Soldiers were stationed here during the civil war. Visitors claimed that they could hear chains rattling at night. The lights would go off and by themselves and doors were closed by unseen hands. Ghostly soldiers can be heard playing cards and talking.

Chapel of St. Peters see Harper's Ferry

Chapmanville, Logan County

Chapmanville East Elementary School is a large, old brick building with a lot of character. Teachers, working after school is out and supposedly empty, have heard strange sounds that seem to always end in a very loud thump! Also howls of pain have been heard. These sounds are reported to have been caused by a terrifying incident one winter in the 1930's. The furnace broke down and it got very cold in the school. The janitor was supposed to fix it but didn't. In fact, the janitor was apparently nowhere to be found. He had disappeared. The school was closed until they could get someone in to fix it. Eventually, some men were hired and they set to fixing and cleaning the old furnace. Imagine their surprise when they found pieces of human bones among the ashes. An investigation found that they were the bones of the missing handyman. Someone had knocked him out maybe and stuffed him in the furnace to get rid of the evidence. The howls of pain are believed to have been made by the poor man when he woke up and burned to death. Further evidence showed that it was his body that caused the furnace to break down. No one has even been convicted for the murder. But the ghost of the handyman still calls out for help in the fiery furnace.

Chapmanville East Elementary School see Chapmanville

Charleston, Kanawha County

A unknown man has been seen passing by a window inside of an empty and locked 1915 bungalow in Charleston's Westside. A search inside found no one. The same man has also been seen walking across the fenced-in backyard at twilight. No one knows who he is or why he appears there.

A house on Greenbrier Street in Charleston is thought to be haunted by a jealous woman. Whenever one owner's girlfriend visited, there would be a series of noises like a battering ram at the front door. A search of the house inside and out found nothing and no one that could have caused the noise. The noises stopped after the owner said obviously that it was just a ghost.

The ghost in the Light Opera Theater on Tennessee Avenue, Charleston, Kanawha County, is not very benevolent. He has been seen on the stage-left side of the former church balcony. Staff members have also felt that his presence is an angry one. They said that, up in the balcony, it felt like someone angrily stomping around and that there was a lot static electricity in the air. Maybe he does not like the type of plays being performed in the theatre.

The Capitol Plaza Theatre in Charleston was built in 1909 on a lot where the old Welch mansion once stood. Artists such as Tori Amos, R.E.M., and other well-known musicians have performed there. The show, "Mountain Stage", was also recorded here. But many people have experienced chills in the theater. The ghost of John Welch, heir to the Welch fortune, is very protective of the place and the actors. Molly Welch, John's youngest daughter, had died of pneumonia at eight years old in 1840. She loved the place and can still be seen sitting in the front row of the balcony. Staff have heard footsteps backstage and seen the back curtain move, but when checking found no one back there.

The State Capitol building in Charleston has its share of ghostly inhabitants. A maintenance man, who died years ago, still goes to work there. The specter of a unknown woman roams the rotunda and halls of the Capitol. No one knows why.

The Sunrise Mansion and its Carriage Trail on the crest of a hill above downtown Charleston, Kanawha County, was originally built by the then Governor MacCorkle in the mid 1800's. Some employees at the mansion believe that it comes to life after they lock up at night and strange things happen. Apparently one night, a police officer meet a strange character when he answered an alarm at the mansion. A man in a red flannel shirt and bib overalls was there with a key to let him in. They searched the house together and found nothing unusual. The officer went back to his car and started his report. Then the real employee with the key drove up! The man in the red flannel shirt and bib had disappeared. Two unknown women, who were murdered and then buried on the site, still seek justice for their untimely demise. The Carriage Trail has a peculiarity. They say a dark spot, no matter how much the sun shines, lies at the second curve for the top of the trail. And, then, Governor MacCorkle, still roams his property now and then.

Watt Powell Park, built in 1948 and named after Watt Powell who financed part of the construction for the park, has a permanent fan - the ghost of an old man. He had lived near by and attended all the games until he passed away in the 1990's and even after as a spirit. The park has since been torn down.

In the 1950's, the old McCory's Five and Dime, now an office building on Capitol Street in Charleston, suffered a terrible fire. Seven Charleston fire fighters died in the conflagration. People say that you can still see the firemen walking in the halls of the building.

University of Charleston in Charleston, Kanawha County has a number of ghostly residents. Dickson Hall was haunted by possibly a little blonde haired girl before it was torn down. Many students reported feeling uneasy in the building and that they were being watched by unknown and unseen persons. They also heard strange sounds but could not find out what was causing them. Geary Student Union Hall at the University of Charleston is also the scene of unusual happenings. Student and staff report strange noises and have seen fleeting shadows as well as having the feeling of not being alone when they was no one else around but them. Riggleman Hall is the same way. Feelings of being watched, strange noises and shadows have been reported. The commotion is attributed to the ghost of a female student who, after finding out she was pregnant, killed herself.

Students and staff preparing for school productions in the theater at Capitol High in Charleston have unseen help. They often, when working late, feel a "presence" and can sometimes hear phantom footsteps walking across the stage to the workshops. Then the lights will dim all by themselves even though no one is in the sound booth and the door is definitely locked. Is it some student or staff member long gone who loved working in the theater so much that they still show up to help with productions?

The Charleston area has a number of great picnic sites. But one is also very popular, they say, with ghosts. The haunted park is on the right hand side of the main highway and just across a small bridge. There was a merry-go-round near the picnic table. A small cemetery sits on the hill behind. Steps made of stone and rocks are set in the hill. People using the park claimed to have heard children's laughter when no children were around. And the empty merry-go-round started to turn by itself. Faint white figures have also been seen playing on it. The merry-go-round has since been torn down. But the cemetery still might exist. Do you have the courage to climb the now overgrown steps to the top of the hill and see what awaits you there? Sure you do!

Spring Hill Cemetery on a hill in Charleston overlooks the city's east and downtown. There are no known reports of ghosts but visitors have experienced some paranormal activity such as what appeared to be ectoplasm.

The Mountain State Hospital in the east end of downtown Charleston was used as a rehabilitation center, nursing home, and hospital. Abandoned for many years, it is rumored to harbor many spirits. But little is known about them.

A log apartment house on South Park Road, Charleston, is haunted by a husband and wife. The man stands outside a window and looks in. His ghostly wife roams around inside the house. Others things happened like the cradle rocking by itself, an unseen woman singing a lullaby, pictures floating off the shelves, lights and water turning on and off by themselves. Apparently a long time ago, a man and woman lived there. The woman suffered from Alzheimer's disease and her husband always looked out for her. But she could not stand having anyone around. He built for her her own house close by and would look in the window to check on her. One winter the man was found frozen to death on the porch and the woman dead in her chair inside.

Charles Town, Jefferson County
A country rural road outside Charles Town has a strange resident. A white cloud shaped like a head and body with a tail has been seen lifting off the ground beside the road. It dissipates and then reforms and glides off into the woods.

Chattaroy, Mingo County
A headless man walks through a creek and disappears under an old railway bridge used years ago as a roadway at Chattaroy, Mingo County. The ghost, wearing a suit and a white shirt with a high collar, was on his way to his wedding and was walking down the track. Then he fell and was beheaded by a passing train. He is still trying to get to his wedding.

Cheat Lake, Monongalia County
Two young women were hitchhiking one night when they were picked up by someone unknown,

killed and decapitated. Their headless bodies were found near Cheat Lake in Monongalia County. To this day, their heads have never been found. Two headless female ghosts have been seen running around the woods beside a local highway, startling drivers. At least, that is the excuse some gave for crashing their cars. Are the two women looking for their heads? If they find them, maybe they will seek revenge on the person or persons who murdered them.

Cherry Creek Dip, Raleigh County

Cherry Creek Dip, just outside Beckley, is the scene of a gruesome re-enactment of a tragic event. A young couple on their wedding night were driving in their white Trans Am through Cherry Creek Dip when another car hit them head on. Both the man and woman died instantly. They say that if you drive through Cherry Creek Dip at midnight on the anniversary of their deaths, you will see their Trans Am drive through the Dip and disappear before your very eyes. A young lady dressed in a wedding gown has also been seen standing on the road near the old antique shop that used to be in the Dip. She, also, will vanish before startled people's very eyes.

Childers Road, Kanawha County

A house on Childers Road is haunted by something unknown. Two red eyes are often seen when the lights are turned off but disappear when the lights are turned back on. It suddenly gets very cold and people have reported that something unseen had jumped on their back. Late at night the dog there would start howling at some unseen thing in the house. Is it the ghost of a cat - a very large cat that definitely does not like living people?

Childers Road see Barboursville

Citgo Station see Dallas

City Park see Martinsburg

Clark Hall see Glenville

Clay County

The Civil War is also still being fought in Clay County. Between 9:30 PM and midnight, the ghost of a Confederate Guerrilla on horse back, who fought with the "Dixie Boys", is still pursued hurriedly along the road by unseen pursuers. Two Union soldiers had bushwhacked him at a crossroad near his home and he is still trying to get away from them.

Clear Creek, Raleigh County

In 1981, a man died of a massive heart attack in the dinning room of his house in Clear Creek, Raleigh County. Either he loved that house a great deal or he does not realize he has passed on, for you can still hear him walking up the steps to his front door. They say that the spot where he died remains very cold no matter how hot it is in the rest of the house. Pets in the house also know he is there as they will not go any where near that cold spot.

Coal City, Raleigh County

Many residents of Coal City, Raleigh County, have walked around the train tracks behind

Independence High School late at night looking for Headless Hanna. She is a ghost of a young girl who was apparently beheaded by a passing train. Some feel that she was invented by parents to scare their kids and stop them from walking on the railway tracks. Then again, some residents say they have seen her.

Coal River see **Alum Creek**

Cole Mountain, Hardy County
For over one hundred years, the folks around Cole Mountain near Moorefield, Hardy County, have seen the ghost light on the mountain. The light bobs up and down the side of the mountain. Do not try to get close to it. It will not let you. It just bobs away. You can watch it best from the road at the bottom of the mountain. Legend says that this ghost light is from the lantern of a slave who continues to search for his beloved master and friend long after he disappeared while hunting on the mountain. The light even chases hunters and their dogs off the mountain.

Cole Mountain Ghost Lights see **Cole Mountain**

Concord College see **Athens**

Copper Hollow see **Fairmount**

Cranberry, Raleigh County
Cranberry, just outside Beckley, is the scene of another track walking ghost but with a difference. In the 1940's, a hermit worked in the mines and lived alone in miner's house behind the company store. He had no friends and was hardly ever seen after work. Then, one day, some people discovered his body burning on the tracks just past the trestle. It is not known how he got there or caught on fire. Today, they say, you can still see the outline of a body burned in five crossties and which remain hot to the touch. And they say that the dead miner still strolls down the tracks every night and a fire starts up around 4:30 AM every morning in the exact same place where he died! Be aware! The ghost of the dead man will touch you if you walk down the tracks and will not let you walk over the spot where he died! They say that he has actually pushed people off the trestle. Wait, that is not all of it! The dead miner was buried in the graveyard on a hill behind Cranberry woods. People swear that his grave remains bare in the winter when every other grave is covered in snow. There's more! There's more! The tracks were removed a few years ago to make walking trails. The ghost is still seen at night. The gravel where his body was found is blackened and the fire still burns there at the same time every morning! The outline of his body can still be seen! Scary!

Cranberry Glades, Pocahontas County
If you go to the Cranberry Glades at midnight, make sure there is not a full moon. Otherwise you may not hear the strange noises people are reporting. Some say it sounds like many people yelling the Civil War rebel yell that resounded on many battle fields. Others heard chains rattling and footsteps on the boardwalk through the Glades. It seems that there was a Civil War prison camp there once. Do the rebel prisoners still hang around?

Cranberry Woods see **Cranberry**

Creston, Wirt County
An old church on the mountain at Creston on Road No. 5 was haunted once upon a time. People climbing up the road to the top reported feeling like someone was following them. Most felt that they were not wanted there. One person was sure she could hear someone calling her name even though her companions heard nothing. Others heard singing and heard a man talking. One man saw eyes all over the front of the church and the door watching them as well as something touching his hair and a chill in his body.

Crosley Station see **Route 7**

CHAPTER D

Dallas, Marshall County
The Citgo station on the Dallas Pike at Dallas, Marshall County, may be haunted but the spirits have only been seen on the security cameras. Black shadows appear on the screen and a dot dances around on it also. If that is not enough, gas pumps go off by themselves even though no one is lifting the handles. Is this a gas and dash ghost?

Dallas Pike see **Dalles**

Damon Cemetery see **Newburg**

Darkish Knob see **Parsons**

Darksville, Berkley County
Darksville - even the name sounds ominous! Go through Gerrardstown, and just past the Elementary School, take a right at the four way intersection. That is Darksville. There used to be an old abandoned clapboard church there. Passersby claimed that they felt chills go up their spines even in daylight. At night, separate, little white mists have been seen floating in and around the old church. The small Darksville church was once filled with local people. Because many were poor, offerings collected at the church were sparse. Some say that what happened was a result of the lack of funds to fix the old church up as it grew older and more decrepit. One cold winter morning, disaster struck! There had been a heavy snow fall and the roof collapsed on the congregation gathered in side. All were killed! the church was of course abandoned after that. But they say the long dead congregation still gathers there to worship.

Davis Memorial Hospital see **Elkins**

Deadman Hollow see **Burnt House**

"Delores" see **Burnt House**

Desales Heights School see **Parkersburg**

Dickson Hall see **Charleston**

"Dixie V. Counts" and her baby, **"Charlie"** see **Harts**

Dorcas Hollow, Grant County
A headless man haunts the Van Meter's small farm in Dorcas Hollow, Grant County, five miles

from Petersburg. George Van Meter, a carpenter from Germany, had settled in Dorcas Hollow in the 1700's. He was killed in a raid by Huron Indians. Rescuers, when they came to his farm, found at first only his decapitated body amidst the burning ruins. His head was found later in a cooking pot at the nearby settlement where the Indians had left it. Apparently George Van Meter's ghost is still wandering around his old farm searching for his head! If you go looking for the headless man, look for the two stone chimneys of the house in Dorcas Hollow off Route 220 from Petersburg. But if this headless ghost is like the Headless Horseman of Sleepy Hollow, then maybe you had better stay home. You do not want to go and lose your head, now - Do you?

Droop Mountain, Pocahontas County

Droop Mountain in Pocahontas County was also a Civil War battlefield. The ghostly soldiers are restless there. Sitting on the battlefield is a replica cannon of the ones used in the Civil War. If you are there on the right night, you will see a soldier sitting on the barrel and smoking a cigarette. Civil War re-enactors have encountered what they thought were other re-enactors. A white horse with a dark figure on its back has been seen late at night. The figure, however, was just a gray mist without a form. Ghostly soldiers have been spotted wandering around a small cemetery behind the Ranger Station in the park. The station itself is often the scene of weird noises, disembodied voices and flickering lights. Several officers from the battle are buried there. A ghostly Union cavalry squad of eight men sometimes block a road in the park or are seen riding through a field. Visitors, touring the site in their cars, have encountered a whole regiment of cavalry while a phantom Union regiment is often seen marching across a field. There is even a headless soldier who wanders the park.

Dry Branch Hollow see Harts

Duffields, Jefferson County

Duffields, an area in Jefferson County, is home to Screaming Jenny. Many years ago, a young lady, named Jenny, of course, was running the train tracks and screaming for she had just learned that her new husband had just been killed. Distraught, to say the least, she did not see or hear the train that hit and killed her. Legend says that Jenny can still be seen running and screaming near those tracks.

CHAPTER E

East Olive Street see **Bridgeport**

East Wheeling see **Wheeling**

Eaton's Tunnel, Wood County
The old Eaton's Tunnel, located in a woods outside Parkersburg, is thought to be haunted. No one has see a ghost but some people entering the tunnel have heard footsteps running on the gravel in the tunnel towards them. No one, as yet, stayed around to see what or who caused them. They ran!

Ebenezer Church see **Louise**

Eleanor, Putman County
In the town of Eleanor, Putnam County, previous residents and people working in what is now an office complex have had ghostly visitors. They often hear ghostly sounds and smell some terrible odors of unknown origin. An unseen rocking chair could be heard rocking in the living room. Shadows shaped like that of a woman are often encounter on the stairs. Orbs and bits of light flit in and around the garden outside at night.

Elizabeth Moore Hall see **Morgantown**

Elkhorn Mountain, Grant County
If you drive across the bridge on the highway at Elkhorn Mountain near Bluefield on a foggy night, you just might encounter the creature known as the Elkhorn Ghost. The tall phantom often appears wearing a red plaid jacket and blue jeans. There is an empty void where his face should have been. He is sometimes seen wearing a hunting cap and carrying a brown paper bag like those that drinkers hide their liquor bottle in. Some who have dared to look closer say he also sports a beard thought his eyes are still, empty black pools.

Elkhorn Ghost see **Elkhorn Mountain**

Elkins, Randolph County
The city of Elkins in Randolph County has a number of ghostly residents. One house across a bridge in the Gilmore area of Elkins is home to the spirit of a young lady who died there in 1860. She is not a nasty one but does like to have fun. Leave anything lying around, she will move it somewhere else. Sometimes she gets a little scary when she makes horrible noises in the night. Every Halloween, like any good ghost would, she throws things at the walls exactly at midnight. This lady is not satisfied with haunting the house, she also roams around on the hill out back. If

you wander around back there, she breaks twigs, branches and sometimes trees to try and scare you off. A huge fire many years ago destroyed three blocks of downtown Elkins and killed twelve people. A lady named Sharah was one of the unfortunate. She did not take it lying down. Sharah still screams her outrage in the Wilson building which stands where the old opera house was before it torn down. If you hang around the train station late at night, a spectral conductor just might walk up to you and tell you that you are going to miss your train! Davis Memorial Hospital supposedly has a ghost that makes noises. But then again, hospitals like schools are always noisy.

Then there is the haunted cottage at Cass Railroad in Elkins. It had been part of an old train logging station. At night, an unseen woman screams and tries to get in the back door. The screen door opens all by itself or aided by ghostly hands. Take your pick. There is the unseen man who likes to whistle - a lot! The ghost of a little girl, who died there, still dashes around a nearby house startling people. If you are looking for a scary spot to vacation, Cass Railroad might just be the place for you.

The prom was set to be held at Graceland Inn in Elkins in Randolph County. Then came the bad news. The Ghost of Graceland Inn was too active. The prom is canceled. This ghost is said to be the daughter of a town founder. Why she did not want the prom to go on is not known. Perhaps she did not have a date for it! Then there is the ghost of a slave beaten to death and buried in the basement. He kicks up a fuss quite often. Visitors to the inn feel that they are being watched and followed. No one wants someone watching over you shoulder when you are dancing cheek to cheek.

Ellenboro, Ritchie County
Back around 1997-98, a teacher at the Ritchie County Middle / High School in Ellenboro and her students were startled by loud voices and knocks that seemed to come from all four walls of their classroom at the same time. There was, apparently, no one on the other side of any of the walls. Strange? Maybe some ghostly students decided to attend class that day and got bored with the lesson.

Elkview see **Big Fork Hollow**

Ethel, Logan County
An abandoned mine on a mountainside in the small community of Ethel, Logan County, is also known to be haunted. Some sort of "eerie presences" are often seen lurking around its entrance. If you dare to get close to the opening or even venture inside, you can hear ghostly footsteps echoing from deep within the long unused shafts. Look hard and you will see a small light that someone long dead waves back and forth in the dark depths of the mine. I dare you to go in further.

"Elva Zona Heaster-Shue" see **Greenbrier County**

CHAPTER F

"Faceless Walker" see **Route 79**

Fairmont, Marion County

Every thirteenth year (which thirteenth I do not know) the ghosts of two boys appear and started screaming, accompanied by the sound of a vinegar barrel rolling in the lake at Vinegar Hill in Fairmont, Marion County. Maybe that is why the hill is named Vinegar Hill? Be careful! If you are the first person they see, they will haunt you for thirteen years. Has anyone been the first person they saw or are you too scared to admit it?

The above story maybe an offshoot of the following one concerning Benton's ferry at the base of Vinegar Hill in Fairmount. Once upon a time, during a terrible thunder and lightning storm, a man was killed when a barrel rolled off his wagon fattening him. Now they say that if you walk up the hill from the old ferry site during a thunder storm, you might cast an eye on two black spots that look just like eyes. If you can hold your ground and not run, you might see a white mist rise up from the old road and cloak the eyes in a ghostly shape. And if you still have not turned tail and run, you might be terrified by the vision of the ghostly form with black eyes turn into a flatten shape of a cackling man. Flat Man will wave for you to follow him or it. And if you still have a small amount of courage to follow, you will see it stagger, fall, get up and dance all the time screaming like a Banshee and clapping it flatten hands together in glee, all the while to the ghostly sound of barrels rolling unseen down the hill around you. At the top of Vinegar Hill, Flat Man will give you a final cackle as a way of saying goodbye and good luck and then disappear before your very eyes. Time for a stiff drink!

About half a mile from Benton's Ferry Bridge on the Tygart Valley River, there is a deep gully called Kettle Run. It stretches from Route 250 to the river. Just across the river from Kettle Run lies another gully called Copper Hollow. A log house called "The Log" used to sit on a hill, and maybe still does, on the south side of the river near Kettle Run. During the Civil War, this area was a route for the Underground Railway. One group of freedom seekers were caught by southern raiders who cut off their heads and stuffed the heads in a kettle. They left the kettle on the river bank while they took the bodies into the woods to bury them. Residents of "The Log" grabbed the kettle of heads and took it across the river up Copper Hollow to a cemetery and buried them. They say that if you stood in the cabin and looked out a certain window you could see pairs of small, mysterious lights coming down Copper Hollow to the accompaniment of a mournful chant. Locals believed that the lights were the heads of the hapless slaves searching for their bodies. When the log house was remodeled and the specific window removed., the ghost lights were never seen again.

In 1914, the old Gaston mine in Fairmount was the scene of a possession by a ghost. One of the miners began to act funny one day - like he was a different person! Many believed he was possessed. A neighbor grabbed his Bible and went to see the possessed man. It turned out that the miner had been taken over by Italian miner who had died in a mine accident two years previous. He was worried for his soul and asked that they send money to a certain priest in Italy and have him say mass with the tabernacle open. When this was done, the dead miner left the living miner alone, who returned to his normal self.

"Faith and Hope" see **Hamlin**

Falling Waters, Berkeley County
The Hammond Mansion at Falling Waters, Berkley County, once a stately mansion, is now an uninhabited and haunted ruin. The story begins during the Civil War, when the owner and his sons left to fight for the Confederates. Their women folk were alone when Yankee soldiers found the mansion. The women, afraid what the soldiers might do to them, took up rifles and defended their home. They were quickly taken prisoner and locked up in the slave house. This is where tragedy struck! the small wooden shack caught fire and the women inside burnt to death. Over the years, strange things have happened there. People could hear voices from unseen persons and often smelled smoke when there was nothing burning. Scepters in old fashioned female clothing have been seen in the building. Ghostly soldiers wander around the grounds. Then there are the eerie mists and strange unexplained lights that hang around the mansion's ruins. An old mill, now torn down, at Falling Waters, Berkeley County, was also the scene of strange happenings. Lights were spotted in the windows of the second and third floors. Eerie sounds have been heard coming from within the old mill. It was a gist mill in the 1800's and may have the site of deadly accidents. Or did someone get murdered there?

Fayette County
What is it about hotels and inns? Fayette County's Blumehaven Inn has both former owners and guests who have passed away and are still haunting around there.

Fifth Street Hill see **Huntington**

5th Street see **Parkersburg**

Firth Street see **Guayandotte (Guyandotte)**

Flinderation Tunnel see **Salem**

Foodlion Supermarket see **Summersville**

Fort Gay, Wayne County
A county grave yard near Fort Gay in Wayne County is said to be haunted but I was unable to find out anything more about it.

14 Mountain see **Route 10**

4th of July see **Martinsburg**

Frame Road see **Big Fork Hollow**

Frederick Hotel see Huntington

Freeman's Hollow, Marion County
Many years ago, a husband was returning home through Freeman's Hollow near Mannington in his wagon with dress material for his wife, when he was killed and his head cut off. His killer was never brought to justice. If you dare to go through Freeman's Hollow at midnight during a full moon, you might get the fright of your life and see the sight of a headless man driving a wagon with a bolt of clothe hanging over the side.

Frist House see **Moorefield**

Fulton see **Wheeling**

CHAPTER G

Gallagher, Kanawha County
Do not walk around Gallagher in Paint Creek Hollow on Halloween night for you just might meet the Late Night Stranger! He is a man wearing a black trench coat and a black hat. When he gets close enough to you, he will greet you amicably enough but his face is just a black blur. Just keep on walking! If by chance you do stop and look back, do not worry, the Late Night Stranger will have disappeared! I wondered what would happen if you tried to keep an eye on him as he passes you. Do you think he might just disappear or still be there looking you right in the eye?

Gallopolis Ferry, Mason County
For two hundred years the remains of Mai Moore House have sat on a cliff overlooking the Ohio River at Gallopolis Ferry, Mason County. The place is not outwardly haunted but some paranormal investigators have experienced unusual and odd feelings about the place when they checked it out for paranormal activity. They claimed that they could hear footsteps following them around the property.

Gamble House see **Moorefield**

Gardiner Hall see **Shepherdstown**

Gaston Mine see **Fairmont**

Gathland State Park see **Inwood**

"George" see **Shepherdstown**

"George Sizemore" see **Bud Mountain**

Germantown see **Wheeling**

Gilbert, Mingo County
A small inn in Gilbert has an invisible patron. Employees say they feel like they are being watched when they are alone. Then there is the vibrating straw holder. It starts to vibrate by itself. Must be a big truck passing, you say? No! The straw holder was sitting on a microwave on a solid base in the back room about forty yards from the highway. Nothing in the place has shaken before or since. Some people feel it might be the ghost of the previous owner still hanging around his joint.

Gilmore area see **Elkins**

Glade Creek, Raleigh County

Few people know that Hawks Nest Park in the Fayetteville area was once a coal mine. A long time ago, many African-American mine workers died in some disaster and were buried in a field at Glade Creek. One of these unfortunate men can still be encounter in the field. Many have seen the ghost of a large black man standing in that field.

Glenn's Run Road, Ohio County

Just about one half mile from Warwood, Ohio County on Glenn's Run Road was the site of a brutal killing. A mother living in a second story house just off the road , for some unknown reason, threw her new born baby into the fire place burning it to death. That old house has since been replaced by a new house. But they say that if you walk down that road you can often hear a baby crying! It is not just any baby in the neighborhood but that poor baby that flung into the fire!

Glenville, Gilmer County

It must be hard for students living at Pickens Hall at Glenville State College in Glenville, Gilmer County, to study with all the paranormal activity there. They hear furniture being moved around, balls dropping on the floor and someone playing marbles. Shadowy forms have been spotted passing through the main lobby. Of course, when they check, there is no one there. But then, the whole campus is haunted , apparently by the ghost of Sarah Louisa "Sis" Linn, who was murdered in the fall of 1918. "Sis" has not been seen but has definitely been heard as she passes through Verona Maple Hall and Clark Hall. She seems to be heading for the cemetery next door to the campus. "Sis" also walks the halls of Louis Bennett Hall. She evens pays unexpected and frightening visits to the tenants. Be careful walking across the grounds between Clark Hall and Louis Bennett Hall late at night, for you may not be alone. Sis Lynn's grave is less than thirty yards behind Louis Bennett Hall and she has been known to wander around the area. The cemetery gate is often found open early in the morning as if someone ("Sis"?) entered through it during the night. Or, maybe they exited the cemetery!

Glenville State College see Glenville

Glenwood, Mason County

There are at least two unwanted residents, maybe more, at the Plumley Mansion in Glenwood, Mason County. A woman in a white dress, who was thrown down a well by her husband, can be heard screaming. Perhaps she is looking for her husband so she can throw him down the well! You can also hear an African-American man, who hung himself in a closet upstairs, hang himself again every night. If you venture into the basement and don't get lost, you just might see blood on the walls. No one appears to know how it got there. They say that a little girl died on the property but, so far, no one has reported seeing her. That goes for the two hundred assorted souls buried under the railway tracks in the area. The property is privately owned and trespassers are not welcome.

Gobblers Knob see Wadestown

Graceland Inn see Elkins

Grade School see **Road Branch**

Grant Town, Marion County
A blast and cave-in in the South Section Main in a mine at Grant Town killed six miners. Their bodies were never found and the section was sealed off as too dangerous to enter. But the ghosts of the dead miners are restless. They say you can hear their cries coming from the sealed off section and they have been seen carrying red lantern wandering their ghostly way through the mine.

Grantsville, Calhoun County
When Cale Bett disappeared, many felt he was murdered. Then a headless ghost showed up in the house he owned in Grantsville in the Little Kanawha River valley and raised cain. Many thought it was Cale protesting his murder. Bett's family tore down that house and built a new one on another part of the farm. The ghost simply moved to a neighbor's house and, once again, raised Cain. Brett's ghost tripped unwary people, blew out lamp wicks as quick as they were lit and unlocked doors. This family abandoned their haunted house and built a new one at the far end of their farm. Brett's ghost was not fazed! It started appearing to people traveling on a nearby highway, trying to get their attention.

Grasslick Road, Ripley, Jackson County
At a farm on Grasslick Road, Ripley, Jackson County, you can sometimes hear a young girl call out ""help me, help me, please, help me!", followed by a blood-curdling scream. If you rush to help, you will find no one. Years ago, a man named John Morgan, who lived in the house, killed a woman. Her sister, who escaped being another victim, told at his trial that she could hear her sister screaming for help. Some visitors say they have seen a little girl running through the fields at the same time. Is this gristly murder being re-enacted in ghostly form in the barn?

Gravity Hall see **Romney**

Geary Student Union Hall see **Charleston**

Green Bottom, Mason County
The home of Confederate General Albert G. Jenkins at Green Bottom, Mason County is a State run museum and is open to the public. It is also haunted. Dozens of visitors have seen swirling gray mists and ghostly figures. Many claim they have felt that they were being watched or that they were not alone when no one else was there. Loud footsteps of unseen person have been heard. Depressions have appeared on furniture as if someone was lying or sitting there. Of course, no one was - at least alive!

Green Bottom Cemetery see **Lesage**

Greenbrier County
Occasionally a ghost is only nasty towards someone who caused its human form harm. Then it seeks revenge and justice! Elva Zona Heaster-Shue, a local Greenbrier County girl found dead in

1897, was determined not to let her death go un-avenged!. Her husband, a nasty man who had abused her, claimed that Zona accidentally fell down the stairs. Zona' mother did not believed her son-in-law and prayed nightly for her daughter to return and tell her what really happened. And that is what Zona did!. She appeared to her mother about two weeks after her death and told that her blacksmith husband had strangled her in a fit of rage and threw her down the stairs to cover up his crime. Her mother went to the local authorities who already had some doubts about the husband's story. He had also acted strangely, not letting anyone look closely at the body and had wrapped a scarf around her neck. The prosecutor had Zona's body dug up and found that she had a broken neck and crushed windpipe. The husband was tried and convicted for murder. He died shortly there after in the West Virginia State Penitentiary. Zona is buried in the graveyard at Sam Black Church. A historical marker on US Hwy 60 at Sam Black Church claims that this was the "only known case in which testimony from a ghost helped convict a murderer."

Greenbrier County Courthouse see **Lewisburg**

Greenbrier Hotel see **White Sulphur Springs**

Greenbrier Street see **Charleston**

Greenwood Cemetery see **Sistersville**

Greenbrier River see **Cass**

Grimm's Landing, Mason County
General McCausland's Mansion at Grimm's Landing, Mason County is also haunted. Visitors to the home have reported that they have heard phantom footsteps and sensed that they were being watched.

General McCausland's Mansion see **Grimm's Landing**

Guayandotte (Guyandotte)
A house on Firth Street in Guayandotte is supposedly haunted but no details are available at this time. Do you know anything about it?

CHAPTER H

Hacker's Creek Hill see **Hodgesville**

Hale House see **Cabin Creek**

Hamlin, Lincoln County
If you are visiting the Isaac Sloane Cemetery in Hamlin, Lincoln County, watch out for the three ghosts that hang out there. One is a woman who likes to sneak up behind you and blow on your ear. Sometimes, she will even whisper in your ear. The other two are babies, Faith and Hope, who giggle and cry and sometimes appear before visitors.

Hammond Mansion see **Falling Waters**

Hampton, Buchanan County
Six miles east of Hampton, a phantom woman continues to commit suicide by repeatedly ramming her car into an old oak tree near a farm. She had had an argument with her boyfriend and decided to end it all permanently. That did not quite work out the way she planned it. After her ghostly crashes, a handkerchief with her initials "JTM" on it, is found in the spot on the same fence - or so they say!

Hanging Rock see **Philippi**

"Hanna" see **Beckley**

Harper's Ferry, Jefferson County
Harper's Ferry in the northeast corner of West Virginia experienced the worst of war during the Civil War as both sides fought over it. It is also where John Brown made his stand against slavery in 1859 and was hung for his troubles. Now a national park, guides dressed in period clothes give guided tours for the thousands of tourists that visit Harper's Ferry every year. There is even a tour of haunted places given. What's that? You did not know the village was haunted? It is perhaps the most haunted site in the state if not the country.

The National Park Service's guest house is thought to be the most haunted. Many visiting Federal employees will attest to that. One such person was confronted by an angry man dressed in a brocade vest with a top hat and banishing a cane. This phantom was standing in the hall at the top of the servants' staircase. When the female employee retreated to the balcony door, she was startled by an invisible hand at her back causing her to stumble. When she turned around, the angry ghost was gone. This lady seems to have some bad luck. She ran into other ghosts, this time a woman in a long, gray hooded dress holding the hand of a little girl. They were standing at the top of the servant's stairs. Without even acknowledging the employees present, the two spirits vanished. A government planner from Denver got a fright in the same house one night. He ran into the angry man in the brocade vest as well as the woman and child at the top of the stairs. All three vanished before his eyes. A researcher napping on a sofa in the front room awoke to the feeling he was being watched. And, indeed, he was! A man dressed in 19th century clothes and carrying a dead man ran by him and disappeared in the hall.

Had enough? Sorry, I am just beginning. A man and his kids used to live on the top floor of another house in the center of town. He was awaken one night by the pitiful cry of a baby coming from his bedroom closet. Then, late one night, he saw a glowing white thing float out of his closet towards his bed before vanishing. Then a tremendous crash shook the building. The man checked everywhere but never found out what caused that crash. Some say it was the fall of chimney during a Civil War battle which crushed a baby.

John Brown used an old log house on the Kennedy farm five miles out of town during his raid in 1859. Today it is a restored museum completed with ghosts. You can heard John Brown's ghost pacing back and forth upstairs and ghostly footsteps going up the stairs. If you listen careful you will also hear long dead people talking, breathing and snoring. Imagine that!

If you take the path pass the church up the hill towards Jefferson's Rock in Harper's Ferry, do not be surprised if you have company you did not expect. A ghost of an unknown little girl in a long white 19th century gown just may grab your hand and walk with you. Do not worry. She is friendly, unlike other spirits you may meet along that pathway. They tend to be a little mean. They may break things, cause you to trip and drop tree branches on you. Have a nice walk.

Visitors to the historic site of Harper's Ferry are often amazed at the recreation, including the actors dressed in period costume. One in particular, John Brown walks down the street with his little dog, poses for pictures for the tourists. Imagine their surprise when he does not show up on the developed pictures. He is not real! You guessed it. He is a ghost! So, if you see a strange, gaunt, white-haired man walking a small black dog on the streets of Harper's Ferry, it could be John Brown himself.

A drunken sailor - how he got to Harper's Ferry is beyond me - often greets ladies and assorted others when they come down the hill at night to the grassy lawn. He wears navy whites but has no hands. If you do not keep an eye on him, he will disappear. Apparently, no one as yet kept a good eye on him.

The Chapel of St. Peters at Harpers Ferry was used as a hospital during the Civil War. Visitors have claimed that you can still hear the screams of the wounded soldiers. Others have reported seeing the priest from that era standing outside the church. The mission chapel is still in use for religious services today. This might be the same church that was hit by a mortar round during the Civil War. They say that this building is haunted by a priest who disappears through the walls. If you stand on the front steps you can hear a baby crying.

A railway runs through Harper's Ferry. In the 1800's, a young girl walking on the tracks was struck and killed by a train. She apparently had gotten lost in the woods and was trying to find her way home. She still is today! Residents living near the tracks have seen a mysterious little girl dressed in a white dress wandering around as if lost.

One of John Brown's men, captured by the townsfolk, was mutilated and left to die. They say he still hangs around Harper's Ferry, perhaps looking for his tormentors.

The haunting of another house in Harper's Ferry is particularly unsettling. The occupants will not go into the basement or the closet by the kitchen. Strange shadows are seen and weird noises heard. Things move by themselves. Paranormal investigators have found evidence of paranormal activity such high power electrical surges in the front yard. Temperature fluctuations were recorded and pictures of the yard and house showed a ghostly like fog and a rain of orbs not seen to the naked eye. Then there is the three hundred year old black locus tree in the back yard. Investigators have had frightening experiences there. One lady, when she approached the tree, felt very panicky and anxious. She thought she saw a body hanging from the tree and then something tightening around her neck. She got out of there quickly - to say the least! Then her ghost hunting friends saw the red welt all around her neck. If some night you are wandering around backyards in Harper's Ferry looking for phantoms and you see an old black locus tree, get out of there!

In addition to the regular run of ghosts in Harper's Ferry, there are a number of ghostly soldiers living there. An unseen army unit, complete with fife and drums, can be heard marching down High Street from time to time. A young drummer boy, killed when thrown out a window by a union soldier, still cries for his mother. If you stay at the Hilltop Hotel, you might be startled by the sight of ghostly soldiers marching through your room and outside on the hotel grounds. Three Civil War soldiers have been seen on Halloween standing near where the old canons were positioned on Bolivar heights. When spoken to, they, of course, disappeared.

Harper's Ferry National Park Service's Guest House see **Harper's Ferry**

Harts, Lincoln County
If you go into Spry Cemetery in Dry Branch Hollow at Harts, Lincoln County at night during a full moon, you might make the acquaintance of Dixie V. Counts and her baby, Charlie. They both died during child birth. When the full moon shines, the dates of their deaths can be clearly seen on their tombstones. Dixie and Charlie also appear wearing white gowns and crying. Dixie seems to be rocking her baby to comfort him. Before you do venture into that cemetery or any place to investigate, make sure you have permission.

"Headless Hanna" see **Coal City**

Heaters, Braxton County
When someone dies in a certain family living in Heaters in Braxton County, ghost lights dance in the family graveyard. The mysterious lights, a red light and a green light in the center with two white lights on either side, dance out into a field and then back into the graveyard. On one

occasion, there were two red lights in the center and three white lights on each side. No one knows what they are or what causes them - only that they appear when someone in that family dies.

Hedgesville, Jefferson County

A motorist was driving near the Spring Mills plantation at Hedgesville when he suddenly struck someone in the road. The distraught driver got out to render aid when he saw a man dressed in a Confederate uniform. He also noticed bloody hand prints on his car. Then the soldier and the bloody hand prints disappeared in front of his eyes! No, he was not drunk! In fact, he was one of many people who have seen this apparition. The phantom is dressed in the uniform of a Confederate soldier with a sword and is bearded. Often, when spotted, he is clutching his back as if wounded. If you do hit this ghost and get out to check, he may not be there!

Hempfield Railroad Tunnel see Wheeling

Hico, Fayette County

An old man used to live in an old shack beside Route 41 near Hico. People staying there overnight used to hear all sort of noises coming from the room in which the old man slept soundly. First there would be footsteps by unseen people. Then there was sounds of a lively party followed by the sound of furniture being moved and lifted and dropped on the floor. Then someone unseen ran across the floor and slammed the door to the bathroom. The old man slept through it all, apparently he was use to it.

Hinton, Summers County

Church goers at the Irish Mountain Catholic Church in Hinton, Summers County, have noticed a cold mist pass over them and settle in the pew beside them. Others have seen a priest appear and disappear in front of the church late at night.

A former prosecutor at Summers County Court House in Hinton still shows up for work even though he is dead. Employees working in the courthouse, that resembles a castle, have heard him walking back and forth across the second floor courtroom. Thomas Reed, the aforementioned former prosecutor and now resident ghost, had an artificial leg. If you stand on the ground floor, you can heard him thumping overhead!

Hodgesville, Upshur County

If you drive to the top of Hacker's Creek Hill in Hodgesville, Upshur County, late at night, watch out for a spectral boy wearing a dark blue coat pedaling his bicycle up the hill. If you listen carefully you can hear the chain on his bicycle rattle. Do not worry about him be out late at night. He has permission - he is a ghost! He was killed in an accident back in the 1920's. If it is a stormy night you may also see a man and his wife on an old horse cart. They are ghosts also! Many years ago they were heading home during a thunderstorm when their cart overturned and killed them. They are still trying to get home!

Huntington, Cabal County

The city of Huntington in Cabal County on the Ohio River is very haunted. Many ghosts reside in its city limits.

A office building in Huntington was once the Frederick Hotel. Built in the early 1900's it was the finest in the Tri-State area until the 1970's. It is also haunted by several ghosts who can be heard walking around and making strange noises during the day. One person, working late one night, was listening to the music played over the PA system when suddenly the music stopped right in the middle of a song. Then a bloodcurdling scream resounded through the building. As soon as the scream stopped, the music resumed right where it had stopped. One man, who had lived in the hotel, claimed that ghosts came into his room at night and argued among themselves. An office on the sixth floor is said to be so haunted that no one rents it for long because of the paranormal activity. The basement of the building is also connected to the haunted Keith Albee Theater by an underground tunnel. Are the ghosts commuting? How many employees working in converted hotel have felt that someone or something other than their boss watching them work?

The bottom of Fifth Street hill in Huntington is haunted! A young couple on prom night were killed in a car wreck and the girl in her prom dress still stands near the bridge at night. This apparition may be the same one that has been reported for over fifty years. A ghostly bride dressed in her white wedding gown was killed in a car wreck after her wedding on a rainy night at the foot of the hill, just before the bridge at the corner of Fifth Street and the boulevard. She stands at the top of the hill, still wearing her wedding gown and thumbing a ride from passing drivers, usually in the early spring when it is raining. It should be interesting if there are two separate ghosts - one at the bridge and another at the top of the hill. Double your fright and double your fun. See two ghosts for the price of one! (Groan)

An unseen presence makes itself known at the Colonial Lanes (west end) at 926 5th Ave, Huntington. She can be heard whispering, slamming doors and walking about. The invisible female often startles people by touching them. A door in the Rebels and Redcoats Restaurant near the bar opens and closes by itself. Phantom footsteps are heard in an upstairs room and singing by an unseen woman disturbs the night. Why is she hanging around the place. Is she looking for a bowling partner?

Female patrons at the Keith Albee Theatre, 925 4th Ave, Huntington, have felt a presence on the stairs to the Ladies Room. This invisible patron follows them to the Powder Room but stops at entering the stalls. Maybe it just needs help finding the restroom.

Some of the locals living in the South Boulevard area of Huntington feel that a house on this street is haunted. Unfortunately, no details are available at this time.

Two small children laugh and knock things over breaking them in the Frederick Hotel. But they are never punished. They are ghosts and how do you spank a ghost? Their favorite playground is the floor above the restaurant. They turn lights off and on and open and close doors. They also like to open the stall doors in the restrooms. Visitors to the hotel have seen the outline of a little girl standing on the stairs as if blocking their way.

A house on Brandon Road in Huntington is haunted. A man came home one day and found his wife in bed with another man. He got his shotgun and killed the other man and his wife and then shot himself. After the murders, the words "Beware to all those that enter!" was found engraved on the inside of a window of the house. The new owners tried to remove the words but failed. When the window was accidentally broken and replaced, the same words appeared again on the inside of the new pane. It is also said that, on a certain night every year, at a certain time, a cold wind would blow in the house and the blankets on the bed would lift off and float to the floor. Years later the house was torn down and moved to the other end of town. The owner kept the window wrapped in a quilt and locked in the garage. One day she went to get it to have a Parapsychologist check it and found the window broken in pieces. The quilt it was wrapped in was neatly folded on the floor beside it. No on knows how it got broken or who did it.

The old main building at Marshall University in Huntington is a great place to believe in ghosts. Its creaky floorboards and dark hallways just cries out GHOSTS! And legend has it that once upon a time, a female student jumped from a third story window to her death. She still haunts the place.

If you are on the stairs at the old Jefferson School on 19th Street West in Huntington, you might bump into a shadowy figure that haunts the old school. Do not worry, you will probably pass right though it. Probably...

The River Park Hospital in Huntington, once a children's hospital but now concentrating on mental health services, has a very dedicated employee even though she passed away many years ago. The ghostly nurse still goes about her duties looking after the patients. Giggling children have also been heard when no children were in the building.

CHAPTER I

Independence High School see **Coal City**

Inwood, Berkeley County
If you hang around Gathland State Park at Inwood, Berkeley County, you might be treated to the sight of long dead Civil War soldiers wandering around the park looking for something. Maybe they are searching for their unit or lost friends.

Irish Mountain Catholic Church see **Hinton**

Isaac Sloane Cemetery see **Hamlin**

Isner Creek, Randolph County
Every year on the night before the anniversary of the Battle of Rich Mountain, you can, if you are lucky, hear the roll of drums and watch soldiers dressed in Civil War uniforms march through Isner Creek near the bridge. No, they are not enthusiasts re-enacting the Civil War. When spoken to, they stop marching and disappear!

Isner Creek Road, Randolph County
Drive down Isner Creek Road in Randolph County, you might see a man, wearing a dark-colored hooded sweatshirt, standing beside the road holding a dog lease. At the end of the leash is a strange looking dog. Strange in that it does not seem to be all there. In addition you may not be able to see the man's face. And if you come back later, he and his ghostly dog may be standing there in or near the same spot. It seems he gets closer to the road with each subsequent sighting. I wondered if he has even made it to the road, let alone across it.

CHAPTER J

Jefferson's Rock see **Harper's Ferry**

Jefferson School see **Huntington**

"Jeremy Walker" see **Barrackville**

"Jim" see **Nutter Fort**

"John Brown" see **Harper's Ferry**

John Second North House see **Lewisburg**

Johnstown, Harrison County
Johnstown is a small community in Harrison County. An apparition called the Black Thing haunted a now disused road and the surrounding woods. Just after the Civil War, a peddler was robbed and killed on this road. His body was never found, only his blood stained coat and hat. The missing peddler was never seen again until the advent of the Black Thing. People passing through that area at dusk encountered a charcoal gray, three dimensional shadowlike figure with no facial features. The creature does not talk but will chase you as far as a creek if you run. A number of years ago, the State Highway Department moved the old road out of the trees to a nearby location. The work crews uncovered a human skeleton in the woods but put it back, despite requests by locals to bury it in consecrated ground and "lay" the ghost to rest. If you walk down that old road in that woods, you just might meet up with the Black Thing. If you run, head quickly for the nearest body of water or the Black Thing just might get you!.

Joy Run, Monogalia County
On might think that a house only a few years old could not possibly be haunted. Only old building are the homes to restless spirits, right? Wrong! A log house less than ten years old on Joy Run near Wadestown is the scene of paranormal activity. To add to the spookiness, there is an old graveyard with almost two dozen headstones in the woods beside the road and an older log cabin that mysteriously burnt to the ground. A smoky white form has risen out of the ground in the basement of the new log house forming into the shape like a human being and then sink back into the floor. The ghostly figure resembling a little girl in an old style dress was spotted looking into a toolbox in the basement before disappearing. A sliding glass door opens and closed by itself. Often a disembodied voice of a little girl cries out "Where is my baby doll?" It may be a co-incident but a doll dressed all in black and wearing a veil had its hair turn green and fall out. None of the other dolls owned by the children of the house were affected. Back to that old graveyard. Investigation revealed that a mother and three children were buried there all in the

same year. Did they all die together? Did they die in the fire that destroyed the old log house?

CHAPTER K

"Kate" see **Kate's Mountain**

Kate's Mountain, Greenbrier County
Many years ago, on Kate's Mountain at White Sulphur Springs in Greenbrier County, a woman, Kate, and her husband were awaken in the night by an Indian raid. While her husband fought the Indians, Kate sought safety for her and her child. After they killed her husband, the Indians raced after Kate, catching her and her child. Both mother and child were scalped. Today, just up the paved road off Route 60 where it turns into a gravel road, you just might see, in the dark of night, a headless woman walking around. They say it is Kate!

If you stand quiet for awhile late at night on Kate's Mountain, you just might hear the sounds of a phantom army on the move. Weird, unidentified lights have flirted around the area and a fog shaped like a human or large cat like animal may also appear before your very eyes!

Keith Albee Theatre see **Huntington**

Kenamond Hall see **Shepherdstown**

Kennedy Farmhouse Museum see **Harper's Ferry**

Kettle Run see **Fairmount**

Kingwood, Preston County
Books jump off the selves by themselves at Kingwood Public Library in Preston County. Something unseen opens and closes doors and makes strange noises. Footsteps made by someone unseen can be heard on the cement basement steps and things move from one place to another all by themselves. I think the public library in Kingwood is haunted! Don't you?

One night, cleaners at the Kingwood Civic Center had just waxed the floor and were waiting for it to dry so they could buff it. Then they heard footsteps coming from the top of the pushed in bleachers. They searched the bleachers and saw no one. The doors were all still locked. They were alone - or where they?

Kingwood Civic Center see **Kingwood**

Kingwood Public Library see **Kingwood**

CHAPTER L

Ladies Bend Hill, Wirt County
Ladies Bend Hill is on an old highway between Morristown and Wheeling. It got its name from a dangerous bend on it and from the fact that in the old days ladies had to get out from the stagecoach and walk around the bend. The drivers thought it was just too dangerous for them to ride in the coach. Many years ago a woman was driving her wagon on that bend, when an ex-boyfriend, hoping to surprise her, jumped out in front of the horses. He surprised her alright and the horses! Frightened, they overturned the wagon, killing the woman. They say that the lady can be seen still on the hill walking or riding horseback while carrying her head in her arms. Her ex-boy, apparently, was filled with remorse - as well as he should- can be heard sobbing for his lost love.

"Lady in Pink" see **Saint Albans**

Lady in Red see **Beckley**

Lakin, Mason County
The Lakin State Hospital in Lakin, Mason County, was opened in 1919 and at first had colored patients. The Boys Industrial School was added in 1957. The place is haunted. A patch of bluish fog sometimes surrounds the place giving it an eerie feeling. Phantom footsteps can be heard on the second and third floor. Doors slam by themselves and something unseen touches people. Visitors have reported cold spots in many areas and a feeling of not being alone and of being watched. Others have heard a deep growling sound, at first like a dog growling, then changing to that of a handsaw sawing back and forth, not through wood but something soft. Some thought it was more a deep and painful moaning. A woman has been clearly heard talking on the second floor. The place is closed now and no trespassing is allowed.

Lakin State Hospital see **Lakin**

"Late Night Stranger" see **Gallagher**

Laurel Creek see **Sandstone**

Laurel Road see **Richwood**

Lesage, Cabell County
Green Bottom Cemetery in Lesage is not a place to wander around in late at night unless you are ready for a very uncomfortable time. You have to find your way at times through a heavy fog. Dress warmly for there are inexplicable cold spots. Then you may also encounter fully formed

apparitions if you are lucky or unlucky - depending on your point of view.

Lewisburg, Greenbrier County

The ghost of a man with a knife chased two teenagers out of the Greenbrier County Courthouse in Lewisburg. The building is connected to the jail and many bad people were tried and sentenced there. If you at there at night you might just hear some mightily horrifying moans. The John Second North House in Lewisburg, Greenbrier County, has a female apparition accompanied with the smell of flowers, even in winter. Sounds came from the only closet in the house but nothing was ever found in it. The story goes that a young lady who loved a soldier was forbidden to see him. He did manage to see her once and talk to her, even though it was only from the corner of the street outside. He had flowers send to her every day until he was shot in the stomach within sight of his love's home and died. Even as a ghost, he apparently still sends her flowers.

Light Opera Theater see Charleston

Lick Ford Road see Witchy Hollow

Little Kanawha River, Wirt County

A few miles down the Little Kanawha River from Creston there is a whirlpool. Once in a while, if you are unlucky enough, you might see a headless torso rise to the top of the whirlpool and then subside back into the water. They say it is the ghost of a peddler murdered by a local barber just shortly after WW1. The peddler had arrived in Creston with a poke full of money and showed it to the barber. The greedy barber killed the peddler and tried to dispose of the body in the river. Apparently he had cut off the peddler's head and had stuck it in a sack. Somehow he dropped the sack in the whirlpool. When he tried to retrieve it, the hapless barber was sucked into the whirlpool never to be seen again. Both bodies were never recovered. The headless peddler is still chasing his head in that whirlpool.

Logan, Logan County

Mame Thurman, a lady from Logan in Logan County, was killed on June 22, 1932 by persons unknown. Though over seventy years have passed, Mame still looks for her killer. Her ghost has been seen walking the woods near 22 Holden where she was murdered.

There is also the possibility that Mame used to ride the 22 Holden bus late at night after her death until the bus run was ended. As the bus near it the end of its run late at night, the bus driver would notice a woman at the back of the bus. She would pull the cord for a stop near the end of the run. When the driver stopped the bus, the woman would have disappeared. When they checked the seat where she sat, they would find the seat soaking wet. Why? No one seems to know. Anyway, the drivers got used to their ghostly passengers, and of course, because they were wary of being called crazy, did not tell anyone about her until years later.

The late Reverend Rush of Logan still inhabits a parsonage there. He often opens the door to the upstairs bedroom to check on anyone resting there. He or someone else unknown walks around in the attic late at night. Then there is the unseen entity that comes in the back door and walks across the floor to the living room. Maybe it is only one ghost - that of the Reverend! Maybe not!

"Lonell" see Weirwood, Pax

Louise, Brook County

Something does not like night time visitors at the Ebenezer Church in Louise, Brooke County. Just ask the ghost hunters who visited it one night. They found that it was as cold as "a freezing grave". The area is dark even when a full moon shines. And there is no sound - it is dead quiet. Nothing seems to move, fly or even scramble among the leaves. The wind seemed to have taken a hike! Something uneasy lurks beyond sight. The something grows stronger as the night gets darker and longer. It will pluck at your jacket, then your hair. Suddenly you hear it stalking you through the dead leaves. The thing may start to throw things at you. Be careful! Look in the church windows. Do you see the red beady eyes? Listen! It sounds like a child in pain crying behind the church! Nothing there - or is there? If you have a walkie-talkie, listen carefully. You might hear a soft "help me!" Then it grows louder until it scream out "HELP ME!" Still want to be a ghost hunter?

Louis Bennett Hall see Glenville

Lowe Hotel see Point Pleasant

Lower Gap, Wirt County

Lower Gap seems to be haunted by a number of ghosts or ghost-like creatures. They say many locals are wary of passing Lower Gap late at night. If you try it, you just might run into a very large dog-like creature, hear screams from unseen sources, see large balls of fire flying around, be spoken to by a white ghostly form and meet a man carrying an old fashioned lantern who vanishes in front of your eyes. Spooky place, that Lower Gap! Some of the phenomena has been attributed to the ghost of a merchant who was robbed and murdered there before the Civil War. If you meet that white, ghostly form that talks, maybe you can ask it what the haunting is all about. That is, if you are not too scared!

CHAPTER M

"Mabel Gardiner" see **Shepherdstown**

Madison, Boone County
In Madison, there was an older house that, when one looked at it, one would think that it was just an ordinary place. Wrong! Many of the owners felt that there was something - a presence - lurking on the property. Often they heard a sound like someone walking into the nearby river. Then they heard a "plunking " sound as if someone was being baptized. Weird! Some feel that it is a spirit of someone who was killed in a church fire on the hill years ago.

Madison Creek, Logan County
People living in a house in Madison Creek, Logan County felt there was something not right with the building. If you went into the bedroom off the living room, the hair would stand up on the back of your neck. Anyone sleeping in the room felt that someone or something was watching them from the closet. At times, that someone or something unseen pulled the covers off people sleeping there. For many years, that someone or something would knock loudly close to the ceiling near the closet. It is a hard place to get a good night's sleep. A walk-in closet in the dinning room had a six inch stain with splatter around it on the back wall. The owners thought it was blood. Whatever it was, they would scrub it hard but it always came right back! Years before, a real nasty man lived in the house. One day another man disappeared and the nasty man in the house was thought to have killed him and buried him in the basement. It is his restless spirit that is blamed for all the strange happenings. The cellar was eventually filled in and the strange events happened less and less. Some speculate what would be found if that older cellar was dug up.

Mahood Hall see **Bluefield**

Mai Moore House see **Gallopolis Ferry**

Main Street Bridge see **Wheeling**

"Mame Thurman" see **Logan**

Mannington, Marion County
Once upon a time, long, long ago, a witch and a warlock lived in the Mannington area. When they passed beyond, they were buried in a local church cemetery. It seems someone or something does not like them buried there. The tombs were turned upside down. If you dare to go there late at night, be prepared for strange noises and something glowing in the woods nearby. Many saw it is the witch who still hangs around and often lets people see her. Will you have the courage to

visit the cemetery late at night? If you do, remember to get permission.

Maple Street see **Reston**

"Margret Blennerhassett" see **Blennerhassett Island**

Martinsburg, Berekely County
On the 4th of July, the city park in Martinsburg is the scene of a strange visitation by a long dead, young Rebel soldier. During the Civil War, the grounds of today's park was often a battle ground where many men died. One man, in particular, may not realize he is dead. Picnickers have seen and smelled a teenage boy leaning against a tree. When told to leave and stop bothering them, the boy just kept leaning against that tree. The smell is terrible like that of rotting garbage, spoiled meat or old sweat. Police are often called but the strange boy disappears before they arrive. The kid is thought to be the ghost of a young Confederate soldier, five feet tall, wearing torn brown pants held up by suspenders, a dirty red checkered shirt, filthy bare feet and a flat top cap with a small brim like the rebels wore. This 4th of July if you are in Martinsburg city park, and you smell something rotten, it just might be that young rebel.

Marshall University see **Huntington**

Matewan, Mingo County
As part of the ongoing labor problems in West Virginia, thirteen detectives working for the mine owners attempted to evict striking miners and their families from company owned home in the Stone Mountain Mine Camp. On May 19, 1920, the situation came to an ugly head at Matewan in Mingo County. Angry miners grabbed their guns and confronted the company men in the streets of Matewan. Sheriff Hatfield and Mayor Testerman sided with the miners. A gun battle erupted! When the firing stopped, seven detectives, the mayor and two miners were dead or dying. The hatred and animosity generated by the troubles at that time still linger today. The ghosts of the dead from the Battle of Matewan still walk the streets of this little town.

McCory's Five and Dime see **Charleston**

McDowell County Courthouse see **Welch**

Meadowbrook, Harrison County
Do not be surprised when driving at night in the Meadowbrook area of Harrison County, you see the ghostly shapes of three men in robes crossing street. The one in front carries a torch while the other two have their hands in their robes. Are they long forgotten monks or devil worshippers rushing to a black mass? No one knows.

Meadowbrook Mall see **Bridgeport**

Middleway, Berkley County
Middleway, a small community in Berkeley County, was once called Wizard's Clip and for good reason. It seems that in the early 1700's, a priest from the Catholic Church exorcised a demon

from the home of one of the first settlers. The village sat in a dark hollow close to a bottomless lake and on the shores of the Opequon River. It was, apparently, an inviting place for a ghost or demon. The story begins with the visit of a stranger to the home of a certain Mr. Livingston during a terrible storm. The owner of the house invited the man in to spend the night. However, the man was dying and asked for Livingston to get a priest for him. Livingston, however, refused to allow a priest in his home no matter how much the dying man begged. The man died at midnight at the height of the storm and was buried in an unconsecrated grave the next day.

Soon there after, strange things began to happen in the Livingston home. A deadly disease decimated his cattle. Weird sounds made by unseen people or things began to be heard in the building . Then all the clothing, linen and horse tackle and saddles were mysteriously clipped in a moon shaped fashioned. The sound of something or someone cutting with invisible scissors could be heard day and night. It was driving Livingston and his family crazy.

One night, Mr. Livington dream about a man who could save him. On Sunday Livingston, persuaded by his Catholic wife and at the end of his rope, attended church. And there in the church was that that man he dreamed about. He was the priest. When advised of the story, the priest agreed to come to the house where he successfully exorcised the demon - or was it a ghost? Mr. Livingston donated forty acres of his land along the river to the church in gratitude. But that apparently was not the end of it. They say that spell cast upon the Livingston family was simply displaced to the old village and the bottomless lake. I wonder if you go by that gloomy lake would you still hear the sound of scissors clipping?

Miller Hall see **Shepherdstown**

Milton, Cabell County
The Mountaineer Opry House at Milton in Cabell County has some performers who will not pass on. When you are on stage you can sometimes hear odd voices from unseen people. There are strange crashes but nothing can be found broken. A ghostly banjo player often practices in the rehearsal room. The performance still goes on and on and on!

Mingo, Randolph County
No one wants to talk about it but there are some unusual visitors to the Mingo Cemetery in Randolph County. They are ghosts - ghostly kids, that is, dressed in old-fashioned 19th century clothes who play in the cemetery.

Mingo Cemetery see **Mingo**

"Mr. And Mrs. Eastridge" see **Bud Mountain**

Montgomery, Fayette County
West Virginia University Tech in Montgomery, Fayette County, is another haunted educational facility. Ratliff Hall is the scene of ghostly encounters and happenings. The phenomena seems to be concentrated on the second floor of the new side of the dorm. Residents have reported being followed late at night by the sounds of invisible footsteps. Curtains in closed windows will

moved in the absence of wind or draft. Doors slam shut by themselves. When the power went off once, a resident caught a glimpse of a fireman standing in the hall. Then he was not there. It seems that in 2000, a fire broke out on the second floor and the fireman keeps coming back to put it out. But no one was apparently injured or killed. Why does he keep coming back. Ratliff is an all girls facility.

Monument Place Mansion see **Wheeling**

Moorefield, Hardy County
The ghostly cries of a baby can be heard throughout the Gamble House, Moorefield, Hardy County. Once slaves were chained to the trees and mercilessly beaten. When the daughter of the house's owner had a child by one of the slaves, the owner killed the child and buried it in the fireplace. The baby still haunts the place, perhaps seeking revenge on it's evil grandfather.

The Frist House in Moorefield was the scene of a grisly murder during the Civil War when Mr. Frist, a Union supporter and his family, were killed by a group of Confederate guerillas called McNeil's Rangers. The house was then used a prison for runaway slaves who were chained to the walls in the basement and left to die. Even though their bones were given a decent burial in 1865 by local town people, their spirits can still be heard screaming and moaning in the basement. Rattling chains are also heard by anyone brave enough to venture down the steps into the darkness. That is not all. On the anniversary of the tragic death of the Frist family, what appears to be blood seeps out of the walls and floor of the room in the house where the murder took placed. Attempts to paint over or wash the blood away are unsuccessful. The blood does eventually fade on its own, only to return on the terrible anniversary day.

Morgantown, Monongalia County
Some employees working in the Morgantown Public Library, Monongalia County, late at night have encountered a ghostly book lover. The apparition is often heard and occasionally seen. Is it looking for a good book to read?

West Virginia University in Morgantown, Monongalia County, is haunted by a number of ghosts. Beta Theta Pi House at WVU has an unusual and unofficial member of their fraternity. Something or someone long gone likes to rattle chains in a lower room. Some feel it is the ghost of a butler of the house who killed himself back in the 1940's. Others think it is the restless spirit of a homeless man they allowed to take up residence in the basement in the 1980's. He apparently hung himself in a small hallway. If you work late at night on the 10th floor of the old section of the WVU Library, you may not be alone! Someone unseen likes to watch students work. Then there is the elevator which likes to open by itself. When it does, listen carefully. You will hear the sound of invisible people getting on and off it. Elizabeth Moore Hall was named after, of course, Elizabeth Moore. She apparently still visits the building in a spectral form. Her spirit has been seen floating over the pool in the basement. Why? No one seems to know. She has also been spotted hanging around in various places in the Hall. Also, her portrait moves around the building all by itself. One day, it is hanging on a certain wall. The next day it is on an entirely different wall. Female students living in the all female wing of Boreman Hall, West Virginia University in Monongalia County, have a ghostly house guest. The apparition of an old lady has been seen walking around the wing. Noises are heard coming from the attic every night at 1:30 am. Someone unseen knocks objects off desks as if they are trying to get attention. Is it a teacher or house keeper too dedicated to leaves her charges even after death?

The cemetery and woods on West Run Rd in Morgantown, Monongalia County, are said to be haunted. This, apparently, makes it a good area for worshippers of the occult. Sometimes, late at night, hundreds of crosses on a nearby hill are illuminated. Folks say its the local witches celebrating their Sabbaths.

Morgantown Public Library see **Morgantown**

Moundsville, Marshall County
West Virginia's most famous haunted site, perhaps, is the West Virginia State Penitentiary at Moundsville, Marshall County. One of the most violent prison in the USA, it was finally closed down 1995. But it legacy of violence, misery and death by foul means or execution still lingers. Prisoners believed that if you died in jail, you never left it. It appears that many are still there in Moundsville. Lights go off and on by themselves. Disembodied laughter is often heard in the prison. Footsteps are heard walking up stairs where stairs no longer exist. A large wheel cage used to safely move the prisoners from the entrance to their cells some times operates by itself. Present day visitors often experience panic and cold chills.

Mountain State Hospital see **Charleston**

Mountaineer Opry House see **Milton**

Mount Harmony, Marion County
Mount Harmony near Paladin in 1935 was the scene of a deadly love triangle. One man was so jealous of a young woman's husband that he killed him by cutting off his head. Alas, the head fell into a well and was never retrieved. The murderer hid the body and lit out for other places. The new owner of the farm moved in and started to experience some problems. He quickly moved giving his reason as hearing every night during a full moon at 8:30 PM a voice cry out "Where is my head?" Even weirder, a voice then calls from the well - "Down here in the well!" The first voice, a bit confused, inquires - "Where? I can't find the well!" The voices would be quiet for a short while and then start their question and answer session all over again. This ghostly conversation apparently went on for years. The farm was long abandoned. I wonder if it is still there and if you can listen in on the ghostly conversation.

Mount Hope, Fayette County
Many years ago, a lady named Princess was murdered in her own home in Mount Hope. For years some of her personal property still remained in house. Locals feel that Princess is still there and is trying to tell people something to get their attention. A woman dressed in a beautiful white dress, like those worn in the 1800's or early 1900s with a high collar and long white sleeves, often waves at startled visitors. You get the feeling someone is watching you all the time. Sometimes, you can catch a glimpse of a figure out of the corner of your eye. Often you can smell perfume, when no one alive is wearing that particular brand.

Mount Vernon, Putman County

The cemetery at Mount Vernon used to have a church on the property until it burnt down. The church door would open by itself. Phantom voices have been heard on the grounds and in the church. A gray colored mist in the shape of a person often drifts among the tombstones.

CHAPTER N

Newburg, Preston County
If by chance you go that way to Damon Cemetery in Newburg, Preston County, say hello to the ghostly woman dressed all in white who likes to roam around the grounds of that burial place.

New River see **Sandstone**

926 5th Ave see **Huntington**

Nitro Street Bridge see **Saint Albans**

Nolan, Mingo County
Once there was a small house in Nolan, where strange things occurred. It was centered on a small room attached to the bedroom. No one ever went into it and for good reason. The door was usually locked but occasionally... Something or someone scary had been seen in the doorway when the door was left unlocked. Skeptical overnight visitors had bed sheets pulled off them during the night. They quickly became believers! Don't go looking for that house. It has since been torn down and a highway built over it.

North Bend State Park, Ritchie County
Tunnel 19 in North Bend State Park near Harrisville, Ritchie County, is one of several old train tunnels. During one of the World Wars, a tragedy occurred that is still re-enacted today. A woman, dressed in her wedding gown, on her way to be married, fell off a platform by the tunnel entrance and was killed by a train. The tracks have been removed and the road bed is part of a system of walking trails. Many believe that Tunnel 19 is haunted, possibly by the Lady in the wedding dress. If you approach the entrance you will experience a definite drop in temperature. Walk through the tunnel and the wind picks up. Then there are the small archways throughout the tunnel. They appear to be lighted by some unseen and unknown source.

North Mountain, Berkeley County
Near Lost City lies North Mountain. Every summer, little, eerie balls of lights shoot straight up from the mountain top. Sometimes some of the balls fly off to the right or left. Speculation has it that these spooky lights are caused by an undiscovered volcanic vent that may run from the mountain to a nearby hot springs. Or maybe, they are lost ghosts.

Number 2 Mine see **Yukon**

Nutter Fort, Harrison County
A house on Bagwell Ave in Nutter Fort is also haunted. A woman's disembodied voice is often

heard. Banging is also heard in the attic. A check found no evidence of anyone or anything up there. The dust was not disturbed. If that does not convince you, one person saw a set of "floating teeth" in her bedroom. How does that grab you! A younger member of the household had an imaginary friend called "Jim", who told him not to be scared. When the family moved, "Jim" did not move with them. Apparently he is still there, waiting for a new friend?

CHAPTER O

Ohley Hollow, Kanawha County
A gray mist-like-figure has been encountered on a little bridge in Ohley Hollow near Cabin Creek, Kanawha County. No one knows who or what it is. Witnesses are usually too scared to do much investigation. Is this the ghost of a colored man hung for sleeping with a white man's wife back in World War II? An old big beach tree sits in the hollow near the Water Plant road. Some people have seen a noose swinging back and forth from the broken branch. Then a dark form takes shape turning into a man swing from the noose. Some have even seen blood dripping from him and hear him gurgling in death. If it is not the ghost of the hung man, maybe it is one of the mob who did the terrible deed and now haunts the area in remorse.

Old Beckley Junior High see **Beckley**

Old Stoco Jr. High see **Besoco**

Old Wheeling Fire Department see **Wheeling**

137 Sammy Street see **Athens**

Opequon River see **Middleway**

CHAPTER P

Paint Creek Hollow see **Gallagher**

Panther, McDowell County

A warlock named Happy Jack and his partner, a witch called Mamie, once lived in a house in Panther, McDowell County, in the late 1800s. Locals feel that they are still there. Lights fly around the house late at night. Invisible cows and pigs moo and grunt. Residents have frequent headaches. Cold spots abound in the house and there is always a sense of being watched.

Parkersburg, Wood County

A house on Agnes street off Staunton in Parkersburg once had an unwanted house guest. A white, gauzy, swirling figure is often seen in a corner of a bedroom. Covers on the bed in that room were frequently pulled off sleepers by unseen hands. The house is long gone but is whatever causing trouble still hanging around the area?

A black shadow of a man running from the east on Ambrose Hill in Parkersburg has startled some late night drivers. Little else is known about it. Have you seen the Ambrose Hill Phantom?

Halfway up Quincy Hill in Parkersburg stands a strange, old house. They say that it felt as if someone unseen was always watching you in the house. An old man with long gray hair has glared out of a bathroom mirrors at the people looking into it! Another ghost, wearing a long dress, has been seen disappearing around the corner. These two spectral visitors do not seem to be malicious but they sure do scare the heck out of people.

If you take a room in the Blennerhassett Hotel in Parkersburg, Wood County, you might have to share your room with a ghost. William chancellor, who built the hotel in 1889 and made it into showplace of the "gaslight era", still walks his beloved halls. You will know he is around when you can smell a strong cigar and no one is smoking any. A young man in ghostly form runs through the halls. Be careful that he does not run into you - or rather through you! It that does not spook you, maybe the ghostly music from an invisible piano might do it.

The first burial at Riverview Cemetery in Parkersburg was in 1801. Today the cemetery is considered one of the most haunted. Strange shapes have been seen around the Weeping Woman statue. Investigators have frequently filmed ghost orbs and other weird anomalies. A disembodied woman can be heard talking and she even calls out your name. Now, how does she know that? A long dead sea captain, dressed in a formal black coat and far from the ocean, crouches over his grave. Why? No one knows! Only ghosts knows why they do what they do.

An old abandoned house, originally a church, still stands on a certain hill right in the middle of south Parkersburg. There are three or more unmarked graves on the property, as well as the known graves of a mother and children. The area is said to be very haunted. Awhile back, there were no houses at the bottom of the hill, only a swampy field, said to be inhabited by the ghost of a woman in white who floated across the field. As for the old house, a ghostly face is often glimpsed in a never used dormer room. A garage at the base of the hill was rebuilt into a home. One night a small coffin appeared in the corner of the bathroom and then disappeared.. A short time there after, a member of the family died. Was the ghostly coffin a portent of pending death? Then there are the strange noises and events that occurred in that house. The faint sounds of old radio shows could be heard coming from the living room. Ghostly footsteps resounded in the hall. The occupants often felt invisible presences both small and large sit on their beds. Nothing else! Just sitting there. There would occur strange knocking and banging noises at all hours in different parts of the house. The living room rocking chair would rock as if someone was sitting in it. An man often startles them when he walks through the hall and disappears. A house across the street seems to be connected with what is going on up on the hill and in the swampy field. Someone accidentally dug up an old casket. When he burned it, a putrid smell fouled the sir. The man died shortly thereafter. Later both he and his dead son shocked everybody when they walked down the stairs before disappearing. The ghost of a little girl often stand at the top of the stairs in this house. To make things worse, a statue's eyes lit up in the dark once and a glowing figure was seen by a wall.

Some times, a ghost becomes almost one of the family. Tinda in Parkersburg did! A house on 5th Street, once a funeral home, was haunted. Strange things happened there. A life-like doll apparently once left a footprint on the marble of a fireplace in a back bedroom. Renters of the house were warned to never unlock the attic door or enter the room. They were not told why. But one family found out soon enough. Needing more storage space, they broke the lock on the attic door and went in. They replaced some broken glass in the attic window. One of the children started to have nightmares about a little girl called Tinda whose mother was a witch and her father had one leg. Tinda was apparently killed by her parents. She had been locked in the attic until one day they pushed her out the window. Then the family found the attic window broken again. They tried to brush it all off as the vivid imagination of a two year old child. It would not be that easy. Other kids in the family started seeing the two year old where she could not have been. They began to feel that it was Tinda pretending to be their little sister. Eventually they got used to her and their sister even began to play with Tinda even though she could not see her. But it was not all fun and games. When the little girl, now older, got a dress and matching hat to wear to church on Easter, she found the dress that Easter morning, covered in blood. No one knew how it got there and washing the dress failed to remove the blood. Tinda continued to play tricks on the family, none fortunately as bad as the bloody dress. Occasionally, Tinda's mother and father were seen but did not cause any problem. The family eventually moved to another home in Reedy. The house in Parkersburg was eventually torn down. Then one night, the mother of the family mentioned above had a dream about Tinda. The ghost was upset as she had no home anymore. Taking pity on the little ghost, the mother told Tinda that the family was moving to Ripley and that she could live with them. Tinda apparently took her up on the offer.

During the Civil War, Parkersburg in Wood County had a number of hospitals to tend to the wounded. When their numbers became too many, tents were set up on top of Quincy Hill where those who were ill or not seriously wounded were treated. But, because of the quick spread of disease, many died there. Some still suffer after all these years. Locals have heard spooky cries and moans and have seen specters roaming the hill.

Now the old Desales Heights School, a Catholic school in Parkersburg, Wood County, is still occupied even though it is torn down. Long ago, a young boy stole a gold cross from the priest. The boy died soon after and the cross was never recovered according to legend. They saw it is still there somewhere. A number of the nuns who taught there were buried the stoned-up walls beneath the school. Before the school was torn down, strange flashing lights and ghostly forms were seen in the darken halls at night. Even today, passersby have seen strange sights on the grounds. Shadows flitting here and there. Misty lights dancing in the dark.

The 4-South section of St. Joseph's Hospital in Parkersburg has a ghost that only acts up on the night shift. It turns over garbage cans and occasionally screams in an empty room.

Parsons, Tucker County
Darkish knob, a hill at Parsons in Tucker County, was part of the underground railway for slaves seeking freedom in the north. Covered with loose rock, many found it steep and treacherous. Nevertheless, they still climbed it. At the base of the hill there was a house that slaves could stop at for the night and rest before going on. One dark night, a young girl, trying to escape from her pursuers, missed the house and rode on up over the hill. At the top, her horse lost its footing and fell down the other side of the hill, taking its rider to her death. Local legend says that on the same night each year that she fell, you can hear her screams!

"Patricia Loy" see Shepherdstown

Pax, Fayette County
If you go to the Pax Cemetery at Pax, Fayette County, after dark, you might see a blue sphere floating around outside the cemetery grounds. Folks say it is the ghost of a young lady named Lonell. Not married, she went to Washington to have her baby as children born out of wedlock was looked down on. Both mother and child died during the delivery. Their remains were brought back to Pax for burial. Because of the bad feeling against unwed mothers, she and her child were interred just outside graveyard. Years later, workers putting in a water line near the grave disturbed it. This apparently upset Miss Lonell's spirit. She began to wander around outside in the shape of a blue sphere. It is also said that a witch names Sally Foster was buried in the cemetery and people have reported seeing form of a woman floating over the top of one grave. Many believe it is Sally. See also Weirwood

Pax Cemetery see Pax

Pentress, Monongalia County
A hundred year old house sits in the woods in Pentress just outside Blacksville. A family with thirteen children lived there until eleven died from unknown reasons. The house itself had no electricity and had thirteen windows across the front. People believe it is haunted. A soft glow could be seen coming from the kitchen. An intrepid investigator entered and found a long skinny

bulb with no casing floating just below the ceiling and giving off an orange glow. A black figure with glowing red eyes has been seen sitting on the side of the road. A white figure has also been seen standing in the middle of the road. A man was hung in a silo that sits up on a hill near the house. A woman was raped and killed by a motorcycle gang there also. People have heard unearthly screams coming from the area. The woods around the house may also be haunted. Hunters walking through them felt that they were being followed by someone or something unseen.

Peterkin Retreat see **Romney**

Petersburg, Grant County
Green orbs have been observed on a mountain top near Petersburg, Grant County. People staying at their trailer on the mountain top were startled by several green orbs that lit up the area. Some of the orbs came right down to the windows of the trailer. The phenomena lasted until 4 AM in the morning. There have been some other reports of the orbs over the years. Are they ghosts trying to get attention?

Philippi, Barbour County
In the 1920's, a preacher in a little church near Hanging Rock, Philippi, Barbour County, killed his overbearing mother and then killed himself in remorse with a cross given him by his mother. Dressed in his black gown, he still appears in that little church standing at the window as if he was looking for his flock to attend his next service.

If you go into Stewart 's Run Road Cemetery at Philippi, Barbour County, at night, you will feel as if you are in a crowd who keep touching you all over. But there is no crowd! Maybe there is! A crowd of ghosts!

Phillips Hall see **Bethany**

Pickens Hall see **Glenville**

Pineville, Wyoming County
A number of years ago, a janitor at Pineville Elementary School got stuck in the boiler room and somehow burned to death. Now, if you are brave enough to go by or in the boiler room at night, you may heard the poor man screaming for help. But, alas, there is no help for that departed soul.

Pineville Elementary School see **Pineville**

Piney Bottom, Lincoln County
Piney Bottom near Harts in Lincoln County is the home of a headless man, dressed in black, who walks around the area. How did he lose his head? Was it over a woman? Is he still looking for it?

Pipestem State Park, Mercier and Summers County
An employee at Pipestem State Park, one foggy night in the summer of 2003, was starting to leave the parking lot when he saw a strange sight emerging from the fog! A man dressed in 17th

Century clothes was riding a solid white horse. The man gave the employee a friendly smile and then rode off down the road and faded into the distance. Then as the employee drove home, he saw strange lights in a roadside field. There, dancing through the ground hugging fog, were a number of ghostly figures dressed as if at a ball. They disappeared when the man looked away and then looked back. Was the man on the horse and the dancing figures just a huge practical joke by friends or others? Pretty awesome if it was. Or where they ghosts? Pretty awesome if they were!

Pleasant Hill, Doddridge County
Pleasant Hill once had a church and a graveyard. A grave shaped mound lay just over the edge of the hill the cemetery sat on. Locals believed that a traveler had been murdered and buried there. They also claim that at a certain (unspecified) time each month when, of course, the full moon shines overhead, a headless man used to hitch a ride on a passerby's horse. If you are traveling on any of the roads near Pleasant Hill on a certain (unspecified) time each month when, of course, the full moon shines over head, and a headless man joins you in your car, please let me know!

Plum Orchard Lake see **Scarbo**

Plumley Mansion see **Glenwood, Point Pleasant**

Point Pleasant, Mason County
The 100 year old Lowe Hotel in downtown Point Pleasant have had their sleep and stay interrupted by numerous spirits roaming the halls and rooms. Many years ago, a woman was thrown into a well by her husband at the nearby Plumley Mansion. She haunts the mansion in company with an Afro-American that hung himself in an upstairs closet. They say, that if you go into the building, you can see the black man hang himself and hear the poor woman scream. Do not go into the basement. They say you can get lost down there. At the least you might see blood on the walls. Even though the electricity is turned off, visitors and passersby are greeted by a lit porch light.

Poor House Road, Berkeley County
A stone house on Poor House Road, outside Martinsburg in Berkeley County, is still home to a long dead soldier from the Civil War. He has been seen roaming the property. The house itself has had a long history. First a farm, it has been used over the years as a home for the poor, a boys home and a state run mental institution. Visitors have experienced trouble breathing in certain spots in the place and have reported a heavy feeling around the kitchen fireplace. There may be more than just a ghost of a soldier abiding there!

"Princess" see **Mount Hope**

Princton, Mercer County
Every morning for many years, the occupants of the Strock Manor in Princton, Mercer County, awoke to the comforting sound of their long passed away great-great grandmother lighting a fire in the wood stove and preparing breakfast.

CHAPTERS Q, R

Quincy Hill see **Parkersburg**

Ramsdell House see **Ceredo**

Ratliff Hall see **Montgomery**

Renick Valley, Pochontas County
Six ghostly horsemen in civil war uniforms have been encounter in the Renick Valley area on the south side of Droop Mountain moving in single file down the road.

Reston, Boone County
After World War II, a "shell shocked" soldier returned to his fiancée and his home on Maple Street in Reston. One night, his mother was popping popcorn. The sound of the popping was too much for the shell shocked young man. It sounded too much like a machine gun firing! He panicked and ran up the stairs jumping out a window to his death. His grieving mother and fiancée moved out of the house after the funeral. Even though that tragic house remained empty for many years, passersby could often hearing corn popping and smell the hot buttered popcorn.

"Reverend Rush" see **Logan**

Richwood, Nicholas County
A great many ghosts haunt a "holler" down Laurel Road at Richwood. One is the ghost of an old man who hangs out on the road near the "cuts" in a rock cliff. They say he once hid some money near there and some naughty local kids beat him to tell them where it was. He died before he did! He is still trying to protect his money. If you drive down the road you may see him walking there. Careful, he may suddenly cut across in front of your car. An old house that burnt down on the road some years ago and a young girl, who hid under a wash tub in the kitchen, was burnt to death. Her ghost, with dark hair and dressed in a white gown, can be seen standing under a pine tree in what used to be the front yard. Sometimes, she comes out onto the road and tries to flag cars down.

Riggleman Hall see **Charleston**

Ripley, Jackson County
A house in Ripley is haunted by the previous family, in particular a little girl who likes to play with knives. A cool breeze could be felt when there was non apparent. A soft-face ghost has appeared at times. The record player would play all by itself and when it was closed and

something put on top of it, the lid would mysteriously open by itself and the object on it would crash to the floor and the music would play. One Halloween, a child's laughter was heard. During a search of the house, a small ghost child was seen in the kitchen playing with the microwave buttons. The ghost child then picked up a knife and chased the family out of the house.

Another home in Ripley was at one time home to a spirit in the form of a rolling blue flame which would appear in the living room and then move from room to room. The mysterious flame often made noises like a whinnying cat. A man named Leander was called in to persuade the spirit to leave. When he approached it, the flame flared up and a loud screech was heard. The flame retreated and Leander pursued it from room to room, until he cornered it in the rear of the house. When he beseeched it to leave, the flame flared up one last time and made a deafening screeching noise. Then it disappeared - never to return!

Ritchie County

In Ritchie County, during the Depression, a ghost with a special message appeared to a woman. Her husband had brought his family back to the family farm when the steel mills closed down in Pittsburgh. He found a part-time job and worked hard to save some money in a bank account for future need. Then he heard that banks were closing and he rushed down and withdrew his money. After hiding the cash on the farm, he told no one not even his wife. But he did promise her that if he ever got sick, he would tell her where he had hid it. One day soon after, the husband was killed in an auto accident. His wife and child were destitute and badly in need of cash. The husband made good his promise! One night he came to her as a ghost and told her where he had hid the money. The next day she found it and she and her child were able to survive until times got better.

Ritchie County Middle / High School see Ellenboro

River Park Hospital see Huntington

Riverton, Pendleton County

If you take a tour of the Seneca Caverns at Riverton, you might get more than you paid for. Small balls of light bouncing along the floor and walls of the caverns have been spotted by tour guides and visitors. Do not try to approach these "balls" as they will scoot away from you. You might also hear doors slamming and see lights flickering off and on. The Caverns appear to be haunted. Why, there is even a "ghost tour" that sometimes follows the human tours around. Do not look over your shoulder as you may not like what you see.

Riverview Cemetery see Parkersburg

Road Branch, Wyoming County

The Grade School at Road Branch is believed to be inhabited by ghosts. Strange but indescribable things as well as unknown people have been seen running across the hallway and hanging around the bathrooms. You can also hear lockers being shut and toilets being flushed in the washrooms. The elevator beside the office runs by itself and the floor indicator lights flash on and off. A ghostly figure has been seen on the grounds for over twelve years. Apparently, a man and his brother lived on the school property before they hung themselves.

Road No. 5 see Creston

Romney, Hampshire County

A black preacher in the early 1970's died of a heart attack while living at Gravity Hall, Peterkin Retreat in Romney, Hampshire County. He loved the Retreat so much that he still hangs out there. Someone unseen plays the piano upstairs. Visitors, opening the door to go upstairs, hear ghostly footsteps creaking on the stairs as the long passed away preacher walks down to greet them. When they walk up the stairs, the phantom footsteps follow them. They have also heard people talking behind locked doors of empty rooms. Unexplained cold spots are often encountered and an invisible presence can be felt as if someone was watching you. Do not be afraid. The preacher's spirit is friendly. He will leave you alone if you ask him.

Room 211 see Shepherdstown

"Rosa" see Berkeley Springs

Route 7/20, Berkeley County

A house at the junction of Route 7 and Route 20 had an unseen inhabitant who liked the furniture arranged a certain way. The occupants could not place anything against a wall by the fireplace without someone unseen pushing it away. Then, when the doors and windows slammed shut by themselves, they decided it was time to move. It seems that the building was a funeral home in the late 1800's. When the house was demolished, the bones of a baby were found in the old fireplace. Was it the ghost of the baby that did not like any furniture near its resting place?

Route 7

A phantom train that makes no noises and just glides along the rails has been seen where the tracks cross Route 7 near Crosley Station. Do you have to buy a phantom ticket to take a ride on it?

Route 10

In the 1950's, a house at 14 Mountain on Route 10 was the scene of a grisly discovery. The family living there heard noises on the stairs like someone was walking up and down them at the same time every morning. They removed the wall under the stairs and found a mummified sheet covered in dried blood, tied at the head and feet with rope. Nobody was in the sheet. It had been apparently moved after being wrapped in the sheet. Years later a body was discovered in a culvert under the road. Was this the body from the sheet? Who was it? Why was the person killed and then moved? Are the footsteps still heard going up and down the stairs at the same time every morning?

Route 12/ 33, Penderton County

There is a farm house about midway between Franklin and Brandywine on a mountain top near the intersections of County Route 12 And Route 33 in Penderton County. The up-stairs apartment is haunted - so haunted that many residents have moved out hurriedly leaving many of their possessions. Many strange things happened that apparently scared them off. Often a crashing noise in the bedroom or kitchen would startle them. When they checked, they found nothing amiss. A phone would ring in the middle of the night in the down stairs part of the house. Footsteps made their way across the floor and someone would answered the phone talking in a muffled voice. The landlady downstairs claimed that no phone rang during the night and no one, of course, answered it. One day, a female occupant of the upstairs apartment was writing a letter when the room became very hot. Suddenly the words "don't hurt them" appeared on the writing paper in thick black ink! The words then disappeared and the room cooled down. One night, while a couple were sleeping, the bedroom window opened by itself, waking them. Suddenly a mist formed in the corner by the open window and drifted over by a crib where the couple's baby was sleeping. The room became hot and a sulfur, rotten smell filled the air. The mysterious mist them moved to their bed and back to the window where it exited. The open bedroom window slammed shut! The occupants always felt like someone was watching them. The apartment was always dark even with all the lights turned on. Whoever or whatever it was would tip over the garbage can in the kitchen, and also glasses, bowls, plates and cans. The bedroom door would slam shut and lock while that rotten sulfur smell would permeate the air.

Route 19, Lewis County
The ghost of a young boy dressed in black is often seen crossing Route 19 near Jane Lew, Lewis County. He killed himself by stepping out into the path of eighteen wheeler. Every evening, he will stand in the middle of the road until someone drives by. Then he will stare at them with a helpless look until they are down the road. See also Alum Creek.

Route 41 see Hico

Route 50, Harrison County
If you are driving along Route 50 between Salem and Clarksburg in Harrison County on a foggy night with a full moon in the sky - beware! Do not stop when you see a woman wearing a red hooded coat with the hood over her head and walking along the road. If you do, you may not like what you see. Some people, who have stopped to offer her assistance, were horrified to see that she had no face when she approached the car window. No one, apparently, stayed to help her after seeing that sight! See also Capon Bridge.

Route 52, Mingo County
If you are lucky and you drive Route 52 into Gilbert near the turn off to Skillet Creek, Mingo County, you just might see a long dead Civil War soldier leaning on his gun or rolling a cigarette while kneeling. This must have been a pleasurable moment in the mist of a battle or skirmish for him, so much so that he still reenacts it when ever he gets a chance.

Route 79, Roane County
My wife and I may have seen the next ghost I am going to tell you about. We were driving on Route 79 between the exits for Wallback and Big Otter. Walking on our side of the road was a man dress casually. There were no houses along that stretch which is raised a bit over the countryside. I looked in the rearview mirror and did not see him, I slowed and looked quickly

back. He was nowhere in sight! He had disappeared! Was he the Faceless Walker of Route 79 that so many have seen? The apparition is tall with shoulder length hair and wears a long brown trench coat. He waves both his arms over his head trying to flag you down. If you slow down to see what he wants, you will be startled to see that he has no head and he glows from within!

Route 97 see Big Branch

Route 857, Monongalia County

If you drive late at night on Route 857 near Cheat Lake outside Morgantown, Monongalia County, do not be startled by the blurry appearance of two girls running back and forth through the woods near the lake. They are not real, apparently. Two college students were hitchhiking back to their dorm on the Evansdale campus in the early 1970's. They disappeared and their headless bodies were found months later in the woods by the lake. Their killer was never found. The two ghostly girls still search the woods for their missing heads, starling drivers on the nearby highway and causing numerous accidents. Or so the drivers say.

Rowlesburg, Preston County

Many years ago, two lovers were eloping on a train because her father did not approve of her marrying a blacksmith. But during the trip, they started to argue. When her husband-to-be became enraged, the woman jumped off the train at Rowlesburg and ran into an empty house to hide. They say that two bodies were found the next morning. The woman was found in the house with her head smashed by a heavy object . The man was found by the train tracks horribly mangles. He has apparently tried to jump from the train to pursue the woman. Every foggy night around the time of year that the hapless couple died, a phantom train comes down the tracks. A ghostly figure of a young woman jumps off as it comes around the bend. The phantom lady jumps up and runs into a house. Then you hear the agonizing screams of someone caught under the crushing wheels of the ghost train. The female specter still haunts the house she took refuge in and is often found sitting on the bed crying in the room where she hid.

CHAPTER S

S.A.F.E House see **Capels Road**

Saint Albans, Kanawha County
The "Lady in Pink" has made the former Sheldon College in Saint Albans in Kanawha County famous. The ghost has been seen in the cemetery where her body is buried and in the building that housed the college and is now a private residence.

A homeless person, drunk, cold and tired, built a fire beneath the Nitro Street bridge on the Saint Albans side of the Kanawha River in early January 2001. They found him in the morning burnt to death. But that was not the end of him. His ghost still wanders around the area.

Salem, Harrison County
A number of years ago, some workers were doing their job in Flinderation Tunnel at Salem in Harrison County when they were surprised by a unexpected train. All but one of the men made it into cubbyholes. The one, who did not, was hit by the train which derailed. Thereafter, and even to today, phantom train whistles, screaming, sobbing and the horrifying sound of metal scraping on metal came to be heard. People walking in the tunnel, now part of a rail trail, often see the lights of an invisible train coming straight at them. When the KKK started to take victims there to lynch them, the tunnel was shut down.

Salem Road, Fayette County
Late at night, a headless man, dressed like a coachman from the early 1800's, has been seen walking up Salem Road, under a street light. Did he lose his head in a coach accident?

Sam Black Church see **Greenbrier County**

Sandstone, Raleigh County
Sandstone lies right where Laurel Creek flows into the New River in Greenbrier Valley, Raleigh County. There is an usual ghost light to be found here. Usually ghost lights travel over land. The Sandstone Ghost Light, however, travels over water from one bank to the other. The ghost light is thought to be actually the ghost of a Union supporter during the Civil War, who ran a canoe service here and was shot by a Confederate sympathizer. He managed to paddle across the river to his home before he died. They say he is still paddling across the river.

Sandstone Ghost Light see **Sandstone**

Sarah see **Bethany**

"Sarah Louisa 'Sis' Linn" see **Glenville**

St. Joseph's Hospital see **Parkersburg**

Saw Mill Road, Lewis County
In the 1930's in southern West Virginia, a man walking on Saw Mill Road near Horner at around 9:00 P.M. saw a large ball of white light hanging very low near him. It was definitely not the moon. The man continued walking and the mysterious light followed right along with him dogging his steps just like a dog. When they reached the forks of Saw Mill Road, the ball of white disappeared. Experts, of course, claimed it was just "swamp gas". But does swamp gas follow people?

Saxon Bridge
Have you heard about the ghost at the swimming hole bridge? The spirit of an Indian warrior can be seen and often heard after dark on the Saxon Bridge. Just park your car on the bridge and wait. Do not make any noise or you may scare it away. The ghost sometimes appears as a bright globe of green light.

Scarbo, Fayette County
The Plum Orchard Lake area at Scarbo, Fayette County, is the haunt of the Beech Bottom Lady" who walks around the area late at night search for her dead husband who apparently drowned in the lake. How she died is not known. Maybe she died from heart break.

Scary Creek, Putnam County
Scary Creek in Teays Valley, Putnam County was the scene of a battle during the Civil War on July 17, 1861. They say it still being fought as battle-like noises have been heard and strange lights are seen sometimes at night.

"Screaming Jenny" see **Duffields**

Seebert Road see **Watoga State Park**

Seneca Caverns see **Riverton**

"707 Phantom" see **Bridgeport**

707 Stout Street see **Bridgeport**

"Sharah" see **Elkins**

Shaw Hall see **Shepherdstown**

Sheldon College see **Saint Albans**

Shepherdstown, Jefferson County

Shepherd College in Shepherdstown, Jefferson County, is another education center that is haunted. In Gardiner Hall, footsteps made by an unseen person have been heard in the middle of the night in a room on the second floor. A cold feeling has accompanied the ghostly footsteps. Some people believe that the ghost in Gardiner Hall is former college professor, Mabel Gardiner, while others feel it is Patricia Loy, the Home Coming Queen. Patricia or Patty died in the shower in a third floor bathroom after hitting her head around 1988-89. She still roams the halls at night and supposedly rests during the day in Room 211. The ghost has been described as a young lady dressed in white with dark brown hair. She is also apparently not the ghost that walks the field outside. Kenamond Hall has the ghost of a mischievous young boy who loves to fool around with the TV and electronic equipment. Then there is George, who died when he fell and hit his head on one of the rocks during construction of the school. He can be seen and heard in the basement still trying to finish his job. Miller Hall had been used as a hospital during the Civil War. With all the suffering and death there, one would expect a ghost or two. There is! A ghost or two. One is a nursing student, who on believing she was failing her grades and not able to face it, hung herself in the attic. Do not bother to try and investigate the attic. It is kept locked to prevent people from trying to go there and students trying to sneak a smoke - or so the administration says.

A woman with long, curly red hair and dressed in a long white nightgown has been seen standing in the windows at the end of the dorm floors of Shaw Hall. When approached, she vanishes. No one is certain why she appears there. Some speculate that she is buried in the cemetery that used to be at the back of the property until the baseball field and the dorms were built. Maybe she was disturbed by the construction as she only started to appear at that time.

Silver Run, Ritchie County

Silver Run in Ritchie County was a small community in an isolated area near Parkersburg when the B & O Railroad was being built. It is now a ghost town. The B & O railroad workers and engine drivers did not like run their trains through the area. The tracks, just before the tunnel there, is haunted by a young woman with skin as pale as the moon, raven haired and wearing a gown. At first, she does not notice you. But, then she turns and casts her cold, deathless eyes on you. Just before the engine hits her, she flies up into the air and disappears into the night! Local say the phantom used to appear mostly at the time of the full moon. No one knew who she was or why she appeared there. A number of stories evolved to explain her. But, one in particular, tells of a woman's skeleton which was found in an abandoned house being torn down in Silver Run. The remains were given a proper burial in an old, nearby cemetery. The ghostly woman was apparently never seen again. Or has she? Some locals claim they can sometimes hear the ghostly whistle of an unseen train coming down the old tracks late at night. Others have claimed to have seen the lady in all her ghastly glory.

Sissonville, Kanawha County

A large spooky Victorian house on Wolf Pen Drive in Sissonville has a mischievous little girl ghost associated with it. The little girl living there was run by a wagon many years ago. Her devastated parents never had any more children. She loves to play ghostly pranks on the neighbors. Her spirit, in an early 1800's dress, often seen walks down the road and loves to lock and unlock all the vehicles in the neighborhood. To add to the weirdness of the house, there is a graveyard above it on a hill. One day, kids walking to school found a coffin on the road. Did it come from the graveyard somehow? Was the little girl playing another prank? An old house on Tuppers Creek Road in Sissonville has been the site of many strange and unusual happenings. One time, the father of a family living there, while working outside, heard what sounded like a mad dog in the house attacking his family. Grabbing a pitch fork he rushed into the house to help them - only to find nothing wrong and no mad dog!

Sistersville, Tyler County

Guests at the Wells Inn in Sistersville, Tyler County, have had some unexpected company. The place is haunted. The sounds of someone writing on a typewriter can be heard in what used to be a second floor office and apartment. Footsteps by an unseen person walk down the halls and doors open and close by themselves. Often guests experience a cold chill in an otherwise warm room.

Greenwood Cemetery in Sistersville can be a frightening place at night. Some nocturnal thrill seekers have reported getting sick when they touch a certain tombstone which was hot to the touch. They were chased back to their cars by moaning white shapes. Just a practical joke by someone? I sure am not going to try and find out!

Soldier's Memorial Theater and Arts Center see Beckley

South Boulevard area see Huntington

South Brooke see Teays Valley Road

South Charleston, Kanawha County

In Thomas Memorial Hospital in South Charleston, Kanawha County, just before a patient dies, a strange blue light floats through the halls. Staff and patients have reported seeing in a number of times. Is it an Angel coming to assist the dying in their journey?

South Park Road see Charleston

South Section Main see Grant Town

Spencer, Roane County

Spencer State Hospital in Spencer, Roane County, recently torn down, was populated by ghostly shapes that walk the halls. Visitors heard chains rattling and moans. Some really sensitive people claimed they could feel the suffering of the dead. Legend says that dead patients were buried in the dirt floor of the room and the rooms were still used. Scary! They say, that when you entered some of the rooms, you could feel the breath of invisible people on your neck. Real scary!

Imagine living in a cave - especially one that is haunted! Just outside of Spencer, Roane County, on Steel Hollow Road, there are a number of caves in the hills. Many years ago, people moving into the area often could not afford to built a house right away. Until they did, they lived in these caves. One family, a man and woman and three children, set up house in a cave just off a dirt road running off Steel Hollow Road at the base of a steep hill. The husband went out hunting to get food for the winter, leaving the wife and three kids alone. While he was gone, the woman and children all developed fevers. She was too weak to even go out and get water. As they got sicker, the children started to cry and cry. The poor woman went out of her mind and smothered them to stop their crying. The husband returned to find his wife rocking the dead children in her arms. All she could say was that the children were sleeping. Her ghost still rocks those "sleeping" children in that cave. The cave may not exist any more as it has been mostly torn down.

Spencer State Hospital see **Spencer**

Spring Hill Cemetery see **Charleston**

Spring Mills Plantation see **Hedgesville**

Spry Cemetery see **Harts**

Steel Hollow Road see **Spencer**

State Capitol Building see **Charleston**

Staunton-Parkersburg Turnpike see **Burnt House**

Stewart 's Run Road, Barbour County
Drivers on Stewart 's Run Road near Philippi, Barbour County, often see a woman in the middle of the road pointing at them. It happens so quickly, they cannot stop their car and run right through her! That's right! Right through her! Not over her! She is a ghost and disappears as the car hits her.

Stewart 's Run Road Cemetery see **Philippi**

Stoco Jr. High see **Besoco**

Strock Manor see **Princton**

Summers County Court House see **Hinton**

Summersville, Nicholas County
The Foodlion Supermarket in Summersville, Nicholas County, has a permanent customer. Sally, a young lady of about eight years, must have liked going to the store a lot. She is still there long after she supposedly passed on. In fact, her grave is below the building. Well, Sally likes to knock things off the shelf. But, do not worry. She puts them all back in their places. However, do not get her angry. She will grab wooden crates and smash them on the floor. She does not clean them up.

Sunrise Mansion see **Charleston**

Swan Cemetery see **Barboursville**

Sweet Springs in Monroe County
One of the most famous spring resort was Sweet Springs in Monroe County. Originally built in 1790 as a hotel, it has been used as a mental institution and a state run nursing home. In the 1940's there was apparently an insane doctor running it. Closed now, it is thought to be haunted but few details are available.

CHAPTER T

Talcott, Summers County

Perhaps the most famous haunted tunnel is Big Bend Tunnel at Talcott, Summers County. It is the site of the legend of the great race between Big John Henry, a steel driver, and a steam power driver. John won the race but collapsed and died as a result. They say that John Henry's ghost still drives steel in Big Bend Tunnel.

Tattletown

Many years ago, in Tattletown, a man, who lost his first wife, married again. Apparently, his first wife did not appreciate it. The mark of a horseshoe appeared on her gravestone. Then the errant man was killed by a kick from his first wife's favorite horse. Legend says that the strange horseshoe mark on the grave stone glows at night. Even more mysterious is the outline, between its arms, of what seems to be two women arguing. The horseshoe has not faded and, they say, can still be seen today.

Teays Valley Road, Putnam County

Back before South Brooke was built in Teays Valley, There was an a pre-war house there with a trailer beside it. The story goes that a family was killed in it long ago and now it was down right creepy. The residents of trailer would not argue with you about that! They had their own problems with the trailer. There were cold spots in it even in the heat of the summer. One winter, there was a knock at the door. When they checked, no one was there and there were no footprints in the freshly fallen snow. A door bell rang once even thought there was no door dell - at that time. Pictures kept falling off the wall and the floor creaked late at night. Oh, just normal incidences in a trailer in the cold of winter? Maybe! Then, how do you explain the smoke detectors going off one at a time and then all together! No ghosts were ever seen. Only all these strange occurrences…. I wonder if any of the present residents have had any trouble or ghostly encounters?

Tennessee Avenue see Charleston

Terra Alta, Preston County

Just outside the small town of Terra Alta, a woman with a white aura around her, appears in a woods before disappearing. Back in the 1900's, she lived in a small cabin in the woods with her husband and her only child. A sudden fire took her child and husband, leaving the woman distraught. She would wander the woods looking for them. A little while later, she died of heartbreak. She still wanders the area in search of her long lost child and husband.

The Log see Fairmont

Thomas, Tucker County
Can a ghost get lost? This one appears to have lost his mine! Thomas in Tucker County was once a bustling mining town. Today it has bars and stores that cater to skiers from the nearby slopes of Canaan Valley. It also has a resident from the past. Tourist are often stopped by a ghostly miner who asks them if they know when the next train to the mine comes by.

Thomas Memorial Hospital see **South Charleston**

"Tinda" see **Parkersburg**

Train Station see **Elkins**

Tunnel Green see **Wheeling**

Tunnel 19 see **North Bend State Park**

Tuppers Creek Road see **Sissonville**

29th Street area see **Wheeling**

22 Holden see **Logan**

Twistabout Ridge, Clay County
Twistabout Ridge near Procious in Clay County is an unusual place with many stories told about it. Once, a man with his pregnant wife and a young girl who was also apparently expecting, moved into the area. When his wife became ill, he hired a second young girl, who subsequently also became pregnant. Now the neighbors began to become suspicious and speculated that he fathered all three children. Then his wife died. The neighbors became even more suspicious when they could not keep the wife's tongue in her mouth as she lay in the coffin. They claimed that this was sign that she was poisoned. After the funeral, the man married the second of the two young girls. She quickly became pregnant again but lost the baby and subsequent ones also. All the lost babies were buried in a small cemetery on a knoll near Twistabout Ridge. That cemetery is said to be haunted, maybe by all those little babies. The house where they lived is also haunted by the apparition of the wife with her tongue hanging out of her mouth. A woman, who lived in a log cabin on the ridge, was stoned to death by her neighbors for some unknown reason. Her body was left under the very stones that were used to kill her. Anyone living in her cabin after that had a hard time. They could not keep the front door closed and could not sleep well for the screaming and sound of the stoned lady running around the cabin. The best story is the one about the haunted mud hole! That's right - a haunted mud hole! Some unknown person was hung from a tree next to the mud hole. Now get this! A ball of light rises out of that old mud hole and a hound dog runs across it ten feet in the air! Large objects came be heard thudding to the ground near the tree but nothing is ever seen or found. Some night, I have to go to that mud hole and see for myself.

Tygart Valley River see **Fairmont**

CHAPTERS U, V

University of Charleston see **Charleston**

Upshur County
Gypsies once lived in an old abandoned house in Upshur County. The locals, who blamed them for any theft in the area, ran them off. Shortly there after, some neighbors were passing by the empty place when they heard a hog grunting loudly. They searched for the hog but could not find it. Many of the locals became frightened of the building and refused to go any where near it. But two stalwart local men were determined to find that hog. Bravely they began to search around the house. Then they heard the hog in some bushes at the back of the building. There, the men found the body of a young child. After the child was buried the next day, the invisible hog never grunted again. It had gotten its message across!

US 50 see **Boiling Springs**

Valley Bend, Babour County
A small mud house in Valley Bend may be haunted by a little child. Occupants of the home have heard a little child calling for its mother. A blue light has been seen floating in a closet. It is not known who the little child is or why it may be haunting the house.

Vancroft-Vandergrift Mansion see **Wellsburg**

Van Meter's Farm see **Dorcas Hollow**

Vernatts Creek, Lincoln County
They say that there is a special cottage that can sometimes be found on Vernatts Creek in Lincoln County if you are lucky enough (or unlucky as some feel) to stumble on it some dark and stormy night. At least one stranger did when he was traveling in that area some years ago. He was wet, tired and hungry and did not know where he would find shelter. Then, there before him was a lantern lit cottage. When he knocked on the door, he was greeted by two lovely women. One was wearing a white dress with black stitching while the other a black dress with white stitching. They brought him inside, fed he and let him dry out. They found a place for him to sleep. Then in the morning after feeding him again, they bid him adieu!. The man found his way to a settlement and told the locals about the kind ladies. The locals looked wary at the news. One local man took the stranger out to the same place where the cottage was. It was not there! There were no ladies about. The stranger was perplexed! The local man explained that he had spent the night with the neighborhood's friendly ghosts!

Verona Maple Hall see **Glenville**

Vinegar Hill see **Fairmount**

CHAPTER W

Wade Elementary School see **Bluefield**

Wadestown, Monongalia County
Gobblers Knob is a graveyard that lies in a hollow at Wadestown, Monongalia County. The ghost of a man, wearing a heavy blue coat and sporting a rifle, appears in a back corner of the cemetery. If you try to approach him, he will up and disappear.

Walker, Wood County
If you walk or jog a certain trail in Walker, which used to be a railway track, you might suddenly fell a cold chill up your spine. Be warned! What you might see next just could scare the shoes off you! A floating woman, screaming "Lord help me!", may just appear in your path. Then she will just as suddenly disappear. No one knows who she is or why she makes such a dramatic appearance at that spot.

Water Tank Hill
Ghost lights have been seen on Water Tank Hill near a small town in southern West Virginia. They have been described as red and glowing like a fireball. One witness, in the 1930's, thought she saw what looked like legs protruding from the fireball. Was it a UFO or a ghost light?

Watoga State Park, Pocahontas County
If you go to Watoga State Park in Pocahontas County be sure to take a drive on Seebert Road at midnight on a foggy night. You gust might see an extraordinary sight. It might even frightened you! A very tall (six and one half feet) bald man, who glows, may suddenly spring up at a fence row next to a cornfield just short of a mile from Route 219. He will stare at you, moving only his eyes as you drive by. Witnesses say he does not just stand up but springs straight up as if his feet are on hinges. He does not bent his knees and his body remains stiff. The apparition has a glow all around it like an eerie halo that lights up the surrounding fog. Has anyone stopped and checked to see what he was? Where the startled witnesses too startled?

Wayne, Wayne County
Something strange happened in a large, white colonial house in Wayne. How do we know? Because it seems to still be happening today. And it has all the classic signs of a haunted house. A room under the stairs remains very cold even in the hot summer. You can often hear the sounds of a violin coming from that room as well as smell pipe tobacco burning. A rocking chair moves on its own. Rust colored spots can be seen on the stairs. When the stairs are painted, the spots show through. Even when than stairs were covered by carpets, the spots still came through. Heavy footsteps by an unknown person pound up those stairs, stopping at the top. Then a door to a room would open and the invisible footsteps enter the room and cross to a wooden dresser. A

drawer opens and someone shuffles the clothes and scratches its fingernails on the wooden bottom. The drawer closes. Then the mysterious foot steps make their ghostly way out of the room. There, they stop. Then there is the chilling sound of a heavy object impacting on flesh and that of a body rolling down the stairs. It is extremely hard to sleep through all this. No one stayed in the house for long. Then it burned to the ground. A trailer sits on the property now. I wonder if its residents hear mysterious footsteps in the night?

Weirton, Hancock County
The Weirton steel mill in Weirton, Hancock County, has been, over the years, the scene of many fatal tragedies. Some of the workers who died on the job still roam the plant. Disembodied voices have been heard. Strange lights have been spotted at night. I bet the security guards do not sleep on the midnight shift.

Weirwood, Fayette County
I would not walk on the railroad tracks from Weirwood to Pax in Fayette County. You might have a companion that could scare the living daylights out of you! You see, there is a headless man carrying his head under his arm who likes to accompany people who walk that stretch of tracks late at night. If you do encounter him, do not worry. When you get to the railway bridge, your headless companion will jump off into the stream below, splashing mud and water on you. The poor headless man had his head removed by a passing train when he was haphazardly walking on the tracks.

Weirton Steel Mill see **Weirton**

Welch, McDowell County
Many years ago, a number of Baldwin-Felts detectives were killed in a worker/union dispute in Matechewan. The sheriff, Sid Hatfield, had sided with the workers against the union detectives. A bunch of the detectives ambushed Sid on the steps of the McDowell County courthouse in Welch, McDowell County. It looks like Sid was none to happy with being killed. Occasionally his ghost is seen walking up the steps to the courthouse.

Welch Mansion see **Charleston**

Wellsburg, Brooke County
The Vancroft-Vandergrift mansion at Wellsburg, Brooke County, has a rich history and is a beautiful building. But it is haunted, they say, by a woman who was hung in the stables by her husband when he found out she was having an affair. Is she seeking revenge or is she trying to warn potential adulterers? A cemetery in Wellsburg is thought to be haunted but little is known of what exactly haunted it and how.

Wells Inn see **Sistersville**

Western Regional Jail see **Barboursville**

West Fogle House, Berkeley County

West Fogle House in Berkeley County was haunted by a ghost who wanted to give away his treasure but no one seemed interested. The ghost, in the form of a old dog, would enter the building and then change into a man. This man - sorry ghost - tried to tell the people living in the home where the treasure was hidden. They were all too scared to listen until one day. One person has sufficient courage to hear what the ghost had to saw. Needless to say, the homeowner found the money and the haunting ceased.

West Greene, Monongalia County

The office for the West Greene School in Monongalia County is in a building separate from the school itself. The building is haunted! Employees have heard strange banging noises and have been startled when the door swings open and no one is there. They have also reported seeing bizarre animal-like creatures. Unfortunately, no descriptions of these strange critters has been passed on.

West Greene School see West Greene

Western Regional Jail see Barboursville

Weston, Lewis County

The souls of long dead residents are said to roam the halls and rooms of the Weston State Hospital in Weston, Lewis County.

Weston State Hospital see Weston

West Point and Kingwood, Preston County

An old graveyard, thought to be at least one hundred years old, between West Point and Kingwood, Preston County, has the apparition of a little girl hanging out there. No one knows who she is or why she is there.

West Run Road see Morgantown

West Virginia Colored Tuberculosis Sanitarium, Pocahontas County

The West Virginia Colored Tuberculosis Sanitarium in Pocahontas County is haunted by the restless spirits of African-American women and men who died from tuberculosis. Nearly three hundred of these unfortunate souls are buried here. In the 1990's the site was renovated but is now closed. Many of the long gone residents still linger. Their burial place remains cold no matter what the weather. Terrifying screams and cries rent the still of the night as apparitions of Black men and women roam the area.

West Virginia State Penitentiary see Moundsville

West Virginia University see Morgantown

West Virginia University Library see Morgantown

West Virginia University Tech see Montgomery

Wheeling, Ohio and Marshall County
The 29th Street area of Wheeling, once called Germantown, has a number of ghosts hanging around. One, in particular, can be found in a house one street over from 29th Street in a house that sits in shadows back from the road. A man, who died, likes to come back to his home on the anniversary of his death, tap at a window and shine a red lantern in. A previous "lady of the house" at Monument Place Mansion in Wheeling has been seen by cleaning staff in various rooms. The staff have also heard music and the sound of dancing coming from the second floor.

Even though the old Wheeling Fire Department building is rented out for other uses, ghostly firemen breathing with respirators can be heard. Someone unseen taps people on the shoulder, shuts doors and walks across the floor.

Tunnel Green or the Hempfield Railroad Tunnel at Wheeling is pitch black even in the bright of day. A man killed by a train has not, as yet, passed on and haunts the old train tunnel. The tunnel is apparently dug under an old cemetery and, they say, the corpses ooze slime down into the tunnel. Do you believe that? Well I am not going to try to find out. Besides the people buried there sure must be unhappy as their rest was disturbed. And it is now used as a pedestrian tunnel? People walking through it have reported seeing ghosts hanging from the ceiling and people walking ahead of them who disappear into thin air. The specter of a young immigrant worker, killed for his money by a friend, floats above the railroad tracks holding a mangled hand before his face and trying to scream.

Wheeling's Main Street Bridge has not just one ghost but two! Years ago, a man getting off his wagon to make a repair was trampled to death by his horses. He often appears on the bridge starting passersby when he asks them where his horses are. A local businessman was inspecting the bridge during its construction and was crossing a temporary one for workers when it collapsed into the river. His body was never found and he apparently has been seen checking the bridge to make sure it was safe.

The apparition of a lady in a black cape stands on her own grave in the Wheeling Peninsula Cemetery in the east Wheeling/Fulton area of Wheeling, next to an old WWII materials factory. Some people think that she is guarding her grave. Did vandals try to desecrate it one night and she scared them off?

Wheeling Peninsula Cemetery see **Wheeling**

White Sulphur Springs, Greenbrier County
Apartment 16 in a certain apartment complex in White Sulphur Springs has a nasty something there. One night, a female resident was taking a bath when she felt something or someone scratching her. Bloody marks appeared on her arms and legs. Then a bad odor like old hamburger wafted through the bathroom. To make matters worse, the room was very cold even though it was warm outside. For four months strange things happened. The toilet flushed by itself and

objects disappeared and then reappear. At the end of the four months, the nasty thing stopped playing tricks and was never heard from again. Do you think it might return? The Greenbrier Hotel in White Sulphur Springs, Greenbrier County is such a good hotel, that, they say, some guests still hang around there long after they have passed away. See also Kate's Mountain.

Wildcat, Lewis County
Another phantom of the road is a woman, wearing a long summer dress and a hat, walks the Wildcat Road at Wildcat, Lewis County. She is reportedly the ghost of a wealthy lady who died in the 1980's. Her ashes were buried on a mountainside cabin on the property that she owned on the dirt road.

Wildcat Road see **Wildcat**

Wilson Building see **Elkins**

Wirt County
A two-story, white house unoccupied since the early 1900's in a holler in Wirt County is haunted. No one wanted to stay in it for long. It turns out that the ghost was not trying to scare anyone. It just wanted help. One night, a group of young men decided to stay in the place for the night. They were playing cards when things started to happen. The front door kept opening by itself even though they kept shutting it. Finally one of the men got tired of it and ordered the ghost to stop. It obliged and the front door did not open again. Well, that ghost must have been impressed by that young man. When he went to sleep, he dreamed of an old man who told him where to find his long lost money. The young man, next day, dug where the ghost told him to and found a small bag. It contained a small number of old coins and some old trinkets. The ghost was happy now and was never heard from again.

Witchy Hollow, Fayette County
Be careful will driving the Lick Ford Road in Witchy Hollow, Fayette County at night. An old car with blazing headlights will come right at you. Just before it crashed into you, it disappears. But just in case it is not the ghostly car, take evasive action!

Wizard's Clip see **Middleway**

Wolf Pen Drive see **Sissonville**

Woodlawn Cemetery see **Bluewell**

CHAPTERS X, Y, Z

Yukon, McDowell County

There is a ghost that hangs around the railroad tracks at Yukon #2 mine. A woman with a bloody face, dressed in a glowing white dress, floats down the tracks. When she spots you, she stops, points at you and screams like a demon out of hell! At this point, you might want to get the H--- out of there!

Then there is this phantom who is really lost. In late June of 1998 , a family in the village of Yukon, McDowell County had a very scary night. They were all gathered for a family reunion and had settled down for the night. Apparently, more than the living attended the reunion! The lady of the house went outside to lock the gate when she was startled by a black figure. She raced for the house closely followed by the apparition. Then it got cold - real cold! That was only the start of the weirdness. White things kept floating over the heads of the children in bed. The black figure returned and tried to smother the man of the house in his bed. His wife, a religious women, rebuked the creature but it did not relent. Finally, the demon went into the bath room and sank down through a crack into the floor. Thoroughly terrified the family gathered together in the living room. There they spied a bear wandering around outside. The house had been used as a morgue whenever there was an accident in the mines. The bodies of the dead miners had the blood drained from them in the basement and then were laid out in the rooms above. Was the black figure a spirit of a dead coal miner who was still upset by his death? They say that it and possibly other ghosts haunt the streets of Yukon, house to house!

Yukon #2 Mine see **Yukon**

SO YOU WANT TO BE A GHOST HUNTER

You want to experience the hair-raising thrills of exploring old graveyards and haunted buildings late at night in the hope of seeing a ghost. But you should not just go off and climb someone's fence in the dead of night. You could get arrested, injured and even killed. You should really join a local ghost hunting group or organization. They usually know what they are doing and have the required experience to make a positive investigation.

If you insist on being stupid and going out with some friends to do a little snooping around, here are some hints that should help you. That is, if you follow them:

Do not go alone!

Do check out site during day. Make sure it is accessible and that you have permission to visit.

Take equipment you will need such as flashlight, first aid kit, cameras, cell phone, etc.

Let someone know where you are going and who with, as well as the time you expect to return.

Do not use alcohol or drugs before and during a ghost hunt.

And again - JOIN A LOCAL GHOST HUNTING GROUP OR ORGANIZTION!

Listed below are links to web sites about ghost hunting.

Ghost Hunting 101
http://ghosthunting101.com/

Guidelines for Ghost Hunters
http://www.hollowhill.com/rules.htm

APPENDIX A: BOOKS TO READ

A Guide to Haunted West Virginia, Walter Gavenda and Michael T. Shoemaker.
Very well-written and definitive West Virginia ghost book.

Coffin Hollow & Other Ghost Tales by Ruth Ann Musick (Original Edition - 1977).
Ghosts and the supernatural in West Virginia.

Elk River Ghost Tales & Lore by Mack Samples (2002).
A collection of tales from the haunted Elk River region of West Virginia.

Ghost of 22 Mountain : The Story of Mamie Thurman by George Morrison (2004).
The story of a woman who met death under mysterious circumstances.

Lively Ghosts Along the Potomac, Susan Crites, 1996. Combines all of the stories from Lively Ghosts of the Eastern Panhandle of West Virginia, More Lively Ghosts and The Littlest Ghosts in one volume.

Lively Ghosts of the Eastern Panhandle of West Virginia.
Susan Crites, 1991. Five very creepy and well-written stories.

More Lively Ghosts, Susan Crites, 1992.
Eight more extremely creepy and unusual stories.

Mothman & Other Curious Encounters by Loren Coleman (2002)

The Greenbrier Ghost and Other Strange Stories, Dennis Deitz, 1990.
Transcriptions of oral tales--mostly contemporary, some traditional--from West Virginia.

The Greenbrier Ghost #2 And Other Strange Stories, Dennis Deitz, 1998.
A dandy collection of first-person accounts of strange, ghostly, and supernatural doings from Appalachia.

The Man Who Wanted Seven Wives by Katie Letcher Lyle (Original edition 1986).
Book about Zona Shue, the mysterious Greenbrier Ghost!

The Telltale Lilac Bush by Ruth Ann Musick (Original Edition - 1965).
Classic book of West Virginia ghost tales.

APPENDIX B: GHOST WEB SITES

West Virginia True Ghost Stories
Collection of over 400 True West Virginia Ghost Stories.
http://wvghosts.com/stories/index.php

West Virginia Ghost Hunters
Includes reports of several investigations and a list of hauntings throughout the state.
www.westvirginiaghosthunters.com/

West Virginia Hauntings
www.wvtourism.com/hauntings/index.htm

The Shadowlands
www.theshadowlands.net/places/westvirginia.htm

More Hauntings of West Virginia
www.prairieghosts.com/hauntwv.html

West Virginia Ghost Sightings
http://www.ghostsofamerica.com/states/wv

APPENDIX C: GHOST TOURS

Beckley
See these turn-of-the-century haunted homes and sites. Tours include the Raleigh County Courthouse, Coal Baron Mansions, and The 1931 Historic Soldiers and Sailors Theatre (interior tour).
Contact info: John Luckton (304) 256-TOUR (8687)

Greenbrier County Ghosts Tours
Contact the Greenbrier County convention and visitors bureau at 1-800-833-2068 for ghost tour information or the division of tourism at 1-800-call wva for area travel information.

Harper's Ferry Ghost Tour
Take the guided nighttime tours through the historic Civil War capitol of Harpers Ferry. Share the history of the town and the tales of the Civil War spirits left behind.
Contact: (304) 725-8019 or visit www.harpersferryghost.20m.com

Lewisburg
Every Friday & Saturday Evening from The General Lewis Inn on Washington Street. Tours on Friday: Combined Tour (mansion & cemetery) - 7:30pm. Saturday: Mansion Tour - 7:30 PM, Cemetery Tour - 9:00pm. Contact: John Luckton: (304) 256-TOUR (8687)

Moundsville Prison's All Night Ghost Hunts
Go on an all night ghost hunt in the halls and cells of Moundsville Prison. Ghost Hunts are open to the public, 18 and over, please.
Contact info: (304) 845-6200, www.wvpentours.com

North Bend Rail Trail Ghost Walk
The terrain is flat and easy, about ½ mile total walk. Hear stories told in the dark as the group continues to slowly travel into the night. The tour lasts about 45 minutes.
Contact: R. C. Marshall Hardware Co., Cairo (304) 628-3321

Parkersburg
Excellent New Orleans style walking tour of the Haunted Places of Parkersburg WV.
http://magick.wirefire.com/
OR: Contact info: Susan Sheppard, Sheppard@wirefire.com or (304) 428-7978,
www.hauntedparkersburg.com

Trans Allegheny Lunatic Asylum (formerly Weston State Hospital)
open to the public for guided tours.
Contact: Rebecca Jordan at (304) 269-5070 or visit their web site at www.trans-alleghenylunaticasylum.com

West Virginia Penitentiary Dungeon Of Horrors
Frankenstein will be your host on this one-of-a-kind Haunted Tour. You will enjoy the comfort of a cell...experience Old Sparkey the electric chair, wander through mazes and get lost in the dungeon of the former West Virginia Penitentiary, one of the scariest places behind bars!
http://www.wvpentours.com

Wheeling
Available from Time Travelers. Tours are 7 P.M. To 9 PM. Nightly. For reservations, contact Dianne at 304-277-5322, Ashley McDonald (304)-277-5322
www.hauntedhistoryofwheeling@yahoo.com

GHOST HUNTING ORGANIZATIONS

North America Ghost Hunters
http://www.naghosthunters.com

West Virginia Ghost Hunters
http://www.ghosthunterwv.tripod.com/

West Virginia Ghost Hunters
Several investigations and a list of hauntings throughout the state. Now accepting members statewide.
http://www.westvirginiaghosthunters.com/

REFERENCES:

Here are some of the many web sites that I researched.

http://ghosthunterwv.tripod.com/westvirginiaghosthunters/id3.html

http://theshadowlands.net/

http://www.Callwva.Com/hauntings/locations.cfm West Virginia tourism wild & wonderful hauntings

http://www.castleofspirits.com

http://www.ghosts.org/

http://www.graveaddiction.com/

http://www.hauntedhouses.com/states/wv/house.htm

http://www.oberlin.edu/faculty/bsimonso/group9.htm

http://www.prairieghosts.com/moth.html

http://www.rense.com/general59/hhbb.htm

http://www.resologist.net/lands215.Htm

http://www.roadsideamerica.com/

http://www.shadowseekers.org/

http://www.westvirginiaghosthunters.com/

http://www.wvghosts.com/

http://www.wvsocietyofghosthunters.com/

http://www.virtuallystrange.net/

Publications:

_____, Sunday Gazette Mail, October 29th 2006, Charleston, WV, "Students Share Scary Stories"

_____, Sunday Gazette mail, October 29th 2006, Charleston, WV "Ghost Dramas"

Blackman, W. (1998). The Field Guide to North American Hauntings. New York: Three Rivers Press.

Bowman, Mary, "Wyoming County History" by Independent Herald, Article published 27 September 1995 "All That Remains".

Hauck, Dennis. (1994). Haunted Places: Ghost Abodes,

Jameson, W.C., Buried Treasure of the Appalachians, August House Publisher Inc., Little Rock 1991

Jones, James Gay. More Appalachian Folk Stories. 1997 McClain Printing Company, Parsons, WV 26287.

Lowery, Terry; The Battle of Scary Creek, Quarrier Press, Charleston, West Virginia, March 1998

ABOUT THE AUTHOR

Author at Harper's Ferry looking for John Brown's ghost!

James Foster Robinson was born in Ogdensburg, New York, USA but grew up in Prescott, Ontario, Canada. He has lived and worked in Ontario, Manitoba, Alberta and British Columbia. In 2005, he moved to West Virginia and married his present wife, Betty. Jim has two books published by Mika Publishing, Belleville, Ontario: Amazing Tales from Eastern Ontario, 1987; Strange But True Tales From Eastern Ontario, 1989. He has also published numerous articles in national magazines, daily and weekly newspapers. While living in Vancouver, BC, Jim was a Feature Writer on Suite101.com for topics - The Art of Storytelling, Storyteller's Korner, Sleep Disorders, Professional Security, and Liechtenstein. In addition, he was a Storyteller both in Kingston, Ontario and in Vancouver, BC, Canada.